THE FIRST LINCOLNLAND
CONFERENCE ON DIALECTOLOGY

Edited by
Jerry Griffith
and
L. E. Miner
Sponsored by
The Department of
Speech Pathology and Audiology
Eastern Illinois University
Charleston, Illinois

UNIVERSITY OF ALABAMA PRESS
University, Alabama

CONFERENCE PARTICIPANTS

Marvin Carmony, Ph.D.
Department of English
Indiana State University
Terre Haute, Indiana 47809

Fred M. Chreist, Ph.D.
Speech and Hearing Clinic
University of New Mexico
Albuquerque, New Mexico
  87110

James F. Curtis, Ph.D.
Department of Speech
  Pathology and Audiology
The University of Iowa
Iowa City, Iowa 52240

Charles G. Hurst, Jr.,
  Ph.D.
Office of the Dean
Howard University
Washington, D. C. 20001

Thomas H. Shriner, Ph.D.
Children's Research Center
University of Illinois
Champaign, Illinois 61820

Paula Menyuk, Ed.D.
Research Laboratory of
  Electronics
Massachusetts Institute of
  Technology
Cambridge, Massachusetts
  02139

Harris Winitz, Ph.D.
Department of Speech and
  Theatre
University of Missouri at
  Kansas City
Kansas City, Missouri
  64110

INTRODUCTION

On March 27 and 28, 1968 seven scholars met at Eastern Illinois University for a discussion of psychosocial problems presented by dialects of English. On the afternoon of March 28, a colloquium was held. This monograph summarizes briefly the discussion held by these seven persons, presents original papers written by them for the purpose of this conference, and presents a transcript of the interchange that occurred during the colloquium.

In 1963, Miles discussed the responsibilities of the speech pathologist in the management of English dialects as spoken by numerous ethnic groups in the United States.[1] His review of the literature cites evidence of the psychosocial impact of dialects on the listener. A major component of this impact is the listener's qualitative judgment of the speech and language of the speaker together with judgments of his social status, economic status, and intellectual capacity. Miles says that the management of dialects requires ". . . unique skills of the speech correctionist and particular attention to phonemic and subphonemic replacements, segmental phonemes, phonology, articulation, interference (as a function of factors in learning two languages simultaneously) —plus a study of the person as a whole in his social setting."

In spite of Miles' position that speech pathologists play an important role in changing dialect patterns, there is little evidence that the profession is taking steps to make its members aware of such responsibilities. With the exception of some few speech pathologists in Job Corps settings, in areas of the country populated by ethnic groups with nonstandard English language, such as New Mexico and Puerto Rican sections of large cities, few members of the profession are actively engaged in the evaluation and management of these language differences. This is not to say that others are not aware of dialects present in their work-communities. They do not know how to approach the problem. They lack orientation to the problem and specific knowledge and training in evaluative, educational, and therapeutic techniques for effecting change in dialect patterns.

The Lincolnland Conference on Dialectology brought together professional persons representing specialties in certain areas of speech pathology and linguistics. These persons have demonstrated a high degree of skill and knowledge in their special areas in the form of research and teaching. Their areas include speech science, dialects, articulation disorders, language development, and language disorders. Outside the profession of speech pathology, descriptive linguistics was represented by a person experienced in the description of dialects. For some, the conference represented their first "in depth" exposure to the problems of dialects. For others, the management of nonstandard and substandard dialects of English is a part of their everyday professional endeavors. The principal purposes of the conference were: (1) to give participants an opportunity to review research dealing with the generative rules utilized in dialects; (2) to discuss various theoretical and clinical approaches to the evaluation and management of dialectolalia; (3) to determine major areas of agreement and disagreement; (4) to consider possible areas for further research.

Each participant in the conference was asked to prepare a paper that would be representative of his area of interest. Its purpose would be to demonstrate to the others the kinds of information he had and the nature of his potential contribution to the problems posed by dialects. Each of these papers is reproduced in this monograph.

During the course of preparing for the conference, an extensive bibliography was assembled by means of a specially designed computer program, which allows for cross indexing by title and by author and allows the user to locate items with certain key words. This bibliography, listed by author in conventional form, is included as a part of the monograph.

As might be expected in a conference of this type, a great deal of ground was covered. Many questions were raised, areas of disagreement discovered and explored, and new directions plotted. An attempt has been made to summarize some of the more important questions and observations formulated by the participants in the course of two days of discussion. On the final afternoon of the conference, an audience of interested persons assembled for the purpose of a question and answer interchange with the conference participants. A transcription of the interchange is included in the monograph. The questions are representative of the kinds raised by professional persons in the field who in one way or another are confronted by dialects. The questions are perhaps indicative of the information needed by them that is not readily available. Providing some of this information will be the goal of future conferences.

Although many issues were raised during the course of the discussions, two points were made that seem to be of greatest significance for the purposes of the conference. The first of these two points is that dialects are nonstandard English language systems that involve much more than differences in phonology or morphology. In any given dialect, there are differences in the phonologic, morphologic, syntactic, and semantic systems when compared to some kind of "standard" English. These differences may have great social, economic, and psychologic impact on the speaker of the dialect if he chooses to move out of his speech community and attempts to live and work in another speech community. The second major point is that when the speaker of a dialect moves out of his speech community into another and attempts to function there, he must often change his language to conform to the system he encounters in the new community. To do so is much like learning a second language. It was suggested then that educational and therapeutic procedures designed to assist the speaker in making the transition from one language system to another be approached along the lines of teaching a second language.

There are serious implications in such an approach for the speech clinician. It would seem that dialects present problems that are similar in some respects, and radically different in others, to the kinds of speech problem usually managed by the speech clinician. The teaching of languages, even English as a second language, has not been within the province of the speech clinician either by training or practice. A question then arises: To what professional group should the management of dialects be directed? If it is speech pathology, what changes must we make in our training programs? Clearly, instruction in second language teaching is not now generally a part of the typical speech pathology curriculum.

A number of important questions were raised, the answers to which would greatly increase our understanding of dialects and give direction to professional management when it is indicated. Some of the more important questions are: (1) To what stimulus pressures does a speaker yield that bring about change in his dialect when he moves from one locale to another? (2) What is the "mapping" between two cultures that have dialect differences? (3) What factors underlie and promote "linguistic snobbery" and how can they be reduced? (4) What dialect differences must be changed if an individual is to advance socially and economically? (5) How do these dialect differences contrast with the kinds of speech problem usually dealt with in speech clinics and schools? (6) What is the generative grammar of dialects? (7) What is the relationship between the use of nonstandard English and scholastic success? (8) What is the "distance" between Negro dialect and standard English? Between Mexican-American dialect and standard English? (9) At what point is maximum competition reached between dialects and standard English?

On April 9 and 10, 1969, the second Lincolnland Conference on Dialectology will be held at Eastern Illinois University. Following much the same format as the first conference, the participants will pursue answers to the above questions and to others that they will raise themselves. One of the principal purposes of the second conference will be to determine the feasibility of a program designed to give a group of speech pathologists intensive short-term orientation to the problems presented by dialects. Some may consider this step premature or perhaps inappropriate. The occasion of a second conference underscores the significance of this problem to our profession. Readers of these proceedings are urged to correspond with us or with any of the conference participants to make us aware of the kinds of problem presented by dialects, procedures currently being used to deal with them, and areas of need as to information, procedures, and materials. Such communication will greatly assist us to deal at future conferences with current problems.

J. GRIFFITH
L. E. MINER

Department of Speech Pathology and Audiology
Eastern Illinois University
January 1970

CONTENTS

1. SOME PHONOLOGICAL RULES
OF AN INDIANA DIALECT*

Marvin Carmony

In referring to scientific theories once felt to be adequate but now displaced, Alfred North Whitehead remarked that older views were not to be discarded but to become "subordinate clauses." Today a good many linguists believe that one such subordinate clause in linguistics is the Trager-Smith system of phonemic notation, once so widely held and so prevalent in textbooks that most notes on American dialects almost necessarily utilized the system, despite defects pointed out repeatedly since its introduction.[1] Accompanying the decline of the Trager-Smith system is a steadily increasing degree of assent to the M.I.T. centered belief that the "taxonomic" approach to phonology—that is, conventional or "surface phonology"—is theoretically inadequate and relatively uninformative.[2] Inasmuch, however, as the full-dress Chomsky-Halle approach, while very powerful and informative, is relatively esoteric, the phonological system dealt with here is discussed largely within the framework of conventional phonemics but under the influence of the generative approach to phonology. This discussion has been influenced by James Sledd's recent description of Atlanta speech.[3]

For the past thirty-five years, most of the serious dialect studies carried out in this country have utilized the *Linguistic Atlas* framework, the primary instrument of which is a six- to eight-hundred-item questionnaire constructed so as to disclose basic features of the lexicon, phonology, and grammar of a given community. Typically, native informants felt to be representative members of three generations and three levels of education are utilized in the gathering of data. As a by-and-large approach to the collection of dialect, the *Atlas* methodology has been of great value.[4]

The description of the phonology of a Hoosier dialect presented here is based upon data drawn from *Atlas* oriented research carried out in Terre Haute in 1963–65, the first comprehensive study of the speech of a single Indiana community. A west-central Indiana city of some 70,000 people, Terre Haute is located on two migration routes, the Wabash River and U.S. Highway 40, the latter for many years considered a marker of the North Midland-South Midland boundary. The study indicated, in brief, "that (1) the vocabulary of Terre Haute is essentially Midland, with a strong admixture of Northern and North Midland words, as well as a considerable portion of Southern words; (2) the pronunciation of Terre Haute clearly reflects the city's settlement and cultural history, the prestige dialect of today stemming from the prestigious and dominant Yankee element of yesterday, while 'inferior' speech is that containing the most substantial number of South Midland features; (3) the degree of both social stratification and racial segregation is considerable, judging from the number of lexical, phonological, and syntactical features with social and racial connotations." [5] In view of the focus of this paper, only the salient features of the phonology will be discussed, the social, regional, and racial aspects of the rules being merely adumbrated.

The use of the *Linguistic Atlas* system of notation, based on a unitary interpretation of American English vowels, permits easy comparison of a given set of data with that of other studies, in particular such a work as Kurath and Mc-David's *The Pronunciation of English in the Atlantic States*.[6] Two additional considerations prompted the use of the unitary system rather than the Trager-Smith binary notation: (1) In some idiolects, the monophthongal variants of the high front and high back vowels occurred more often than the diphthongal variants; (2) Upgliding or fronting diphthongs, some of them clearly variants of the lax vowels of *bit* and *bet,* occurred frequently in the records of some of the informants. The Trager-Smith system can hardly accommodate the modifications necessitated in order to indicate the difference between, say, *special* [spɛ́ɛˆš(ʉ*)ɫ] and *spatial* [speeˆš̌ʉɫ], both of the stressed nuclei being transcribed as /ey/. A corresponding pronunciation of /ɪ/ also occurs.

The "phonemes" of Terre Haute English, the distinctive points "in a network of interlocking differences of sound" [7] in the speech of the community, may be indicated for the vowels as follows:

Tense	i		u
	e		o
	ai		ɔ
	æ ʉ		ɔ i
Lax	ɪ		u
	ɛ		ʌ
	æ		a
Reduced		ə	

The tense vowel /i/ of *beat* is matched by the lax vowel /ɪ/

* Preferred phonetic symbol not available.

of *bit*. The tense-lax dichotomy likewise relates the /e/ of *bait* to the /ɛ/ of *bet,* the /u/ of *boot* to the /ʊ/ of *book,* the /o/ of *boat* to the /ʌ/ of *but*. /a/, phonetically the vowel of *lot* and *cot* in Terre Haute speech, is related to /ɔ/, the usual vowel of *caught*. The reduced /ə/ is the usual vowel occurring in the unstressed syllables of such words as *bucket* and *pencil*.

LAX VOWELS

/ɪ/

The principal allophone of /ɪ/, the vowel of *bit,* is [ɪ], usually slightly more lax than the version of this vowel most frequently heard in southern Indiana and other parts of the southern Middle West. This allophone may occur in any environment in which the phoneme /ɪ/ occurs, even under change of pitch and before voiced consonants, where a lengthened version is heard. Under change of pitch, however, an ingliding allophone [ɪə] occurs very frequently, appearing in the Terre Haute records before all consonants except the velars /k/ and /g/, the velar nasal /ŋ/, and the alveopalatals /š/ and /ž/. Before these consonants, a lax upgliding allophone [ɪɪˆ] is in complementary distribution with [ɪ], almost to the exclusion of the ingliding allophone.

It is possible, of course, to comment more succinctly on the pronunciation of /ɪ/. Thus the loosely stated and unordered "rules" for the pronunciation of /ɪ/ may be outlined as follows:

(1) [ɪ] may occur in all environments in which /ɪ/ occurs, in terms, of course, of the whole dialect. [ɪ] is lengthened before voiced consonants and, under changing pitch, before unvoiced consonants.

(2) [ɪə] occurs optionally under changing pitch before all the consonants except, for all practical purposes, /k/, /g/, /š/, /ž/, and /ŋ/.

(3) [ɪɪ̂] occurs optionally before /g/, /š/, /ž/, and /ŋ/.

So far as I have observed in the speech of Terre Hauteans, *dinner* and *sister* never have the high central [ɨ] so common in the South. However, *little* quite often has [ɨ], more often a centralized /ʊ/:[ʊ̈], or fronted /ʊ/:[ʊ̈]. *Children* often has /ʊ/ in the stressed syllable. The centralized /ʊ/, sometimes unrounded to a back [ɨ], occurs so frequently in free variation or complementary distribution with [ʊ] in palatal environments that [ɨ] is taken as an allophone of /ʊ/ in the dialect.

The occurrence of /ʊ/ in the pronunciation of such words as *little* and *children* reflects the velarity, that is, the *gravity* of [l].[8] The occurrence of the lax upgliding diphthong of /ɪ/, as in *dish* [dɪɪ̂š], reflects palatalized versions of the compact consonants /š/, /ž/ (rare), /g/, and /ŋ/. It is likely that such lax upgliding allophones occur only in regions where the neutralization of /i/ and /ɪ/ occasionally occurs, as in *dish* [diš] and *fish* [fiš]. They may, in fact, account for the neutralization itself, which is relatively uncommon in Terre Haute but a prominent feature of the speech of West Terre Haute, two miles west across the Wabash River. A possible reflex of the pronunciation of *dish* and *fish* with the vowel of *beat* is the pronunciation of such words as *appreciate* and *deletion* with the vowel of *kit*.

/ε/

The pronunciations of the vowel of *bet* closely parallel those of /ε/, the vowel of *bit*. In the dialect as a whole, although not in certain idiolects, the monophthong [ε] occurs anywhere that /ɛ/ occurs. It is lengthened before voiced consonants and, under changing pitch, before unvoiced consonants. Under changing pitch, an inglide occurs optionally before labials, interdentals, and alveolars, including /l/ and /r/, as in *cob web*, [kʼab wɛəb], *Seth* [sɛəθ], *deaf* [dɛəf], and *hotel* [hótʼɛɯɬ]. Before the remaining consonants, except the two affricates and /k/, an upgliding version of /ɛ/ occurs, as in *expression* [ɪksprʼɛɪšən], *fresh* [frɛɪˇš], and *keg* [kɛɪˆgˌ]. The upgliding allophone is thus in complementary variation with the ingliding allophone and is in free variation with the monophthong. Apparently the affricates /č/ and /ǰ/ rarely figure in intrusive glides.

As in the case of the upgliding version of /ɪ/, the palatal glide following /ɛ/ appears to be related to the neutralization of the /e/:/ɛ/ contrast before the palatals /š/ and /ž/ and the velars /g/ and /ŋ/. One informant apparently has only the /e/ of *bait* before these consonants. In most cases, however, the upgliding allophone of /ɛ/ alternates with the monophthongal variant, the pattern of distribution being related to both the age and the education of the informants. In cultivated speech, [ɛɛˆ] occurs more often before /g/ than elsewhere and is limited to this environment in some idiolects. The velarity or gravity of /ŋ/ may account for the lowering of /ɪ/ to /ɛ/ in the pronunciation of any number of /ɪ/ words, such as *bring, thing,* and *sing.* The allophone of the resulting /ɛ/ is often the upgliding [ɛɛˆ], related to [ŋˌ], a fronted version of /ŋ/. Inasmuch as any form pronounced with the upgliding allophone is subject to the neutralization option, one hears in certain segments of Terre Haute speech the occasional pronunciation of *sing* as /seŋ/, *thing* as [θeŋ], and so on, pronunciations occurring very frequently in

Southern Indiana and elsewhere in the southern Middle West.

/æ/

The pronunciation of the vowel of *bat* and *map* involves a monophthong [æ], an ingliding diphthong [æə], and an upgliding allophone [æɪ]. As in the case of the other lax vowels, the monophthong [æ] is virtually regular before the affricates and /k/, as in *catch* [kʼæč] and *sack* [sæk]. Under changing pitch, a short schwa-like glide may intrude before the labials, alveolars, and interdentals, in descending order of frequency, as in *lamp* [læəmp], *glass* [glæəs], and *bath* [bæəθ]. A lax upgliding variant of /æ/, matching the upgliding versions of /ɪ/ and /ɛ/, occurs optionally before /š/, /ž/, /g/, and /ŋ/, as in *Wabash* [wɒbæɪš], *paper bag* [bæeˆgɟ], and *rang* [ræɪ̃ɟ]. No instances of this allophone occur in the Terre Haute records before /ž/, but the writer has heard it a few times in common speech in the pronunciation of *azure* [æʼɪžɵr]. The neutralization of the /æ/:/e/ distinction in one or more of the environments in which [æɪ] occurs is apparently a rarity in Terre Haute speech. The writer has noted it, however, in one local inhabitant's pronunciation of *cash* as [kʼeɪ̂š], using the vowel of *bait*.[9]

It will be seen that a consolidation of the rules for lax front vowels may be achieved. Without reference to their numerous social correlations, the rules may be stated as follows:

(1) The lax front vowels /ɪ/, /ɛ/, and /æ/ are lengthened somewhat before voiced consonants and, under changing pitch, before unvoiced consonants.

(2) Under changing pitch a schwa or velar glide [10] intrudes optionally before labials, alveolars, and interdentals. These glides are usually quite short.

(3) More often under changing pitch but sometimes under level pitch, a palatal glide intrudes before /š/, /ž/, /g/, and /ŋ/.

(4) Under the influence of the palatal glide, the lax vowels /ɪ/ and /ɛ/ may be raised to the corresponding tense vowels /i/ and /e/.

The latter rule accounts for the pronunciation of *dish* with the vowel of *beat* and *eggs* with the vowel of *bait*. Although the form *can't* does not occur in the Terre Haute records as [k'æɪnt], the South Midland and Southern extension of the palatal glide "rule" to the alveolars accounts not only for [k'æmt], but also for the raising of /æ/ to /ɛ/ and /e/, thus producing *can't* as /kent/. Not surprisingly, the latter pronunciation does not occur in the Terre Haute records.

/ʌ/

The principal allophone of the vowel of *bucket* is [ʌ], a centered, mid-back unrounded lax vowel. Optionally, it is somewhat fronted in alveolar and palatal, i.e., acute environments, as in *Sunday* [s'ʌ˄ndiˇ] and *such* [sʌč̣]. The velarity of a following /l/ may account for the backing and rounding of [ʌ] to [ɔˇ] in such words as *Hulman* [hɔˇɫmən] *Center* and *gulf* [gɔˇɫf].

The j glide occurring after the lax front vowels intrudes after /ʌ/ before /š/ and /ǰ/ in the speech of some of the informants. [ʌɪ] occurs in *mush* [mʌɪš] and in *judge* [ǰʌ˄ɪǰ] in the oldest Negro speech and in the speech of one white informant with substantial southern Indiana roots. The oldest Negro informant does not have the intrusive glide before /š/ in pronouncing *brush,* but instead utilizes the mid-front lax vowel /ɛ/. It seems reasonable to assume that the occurrence of the vowel of *bet* in *brush* is the result of what might be called intrusive-i mutation, the process ostensibly involved in the changes previously noted. Under the influence of the j glide [ʌ] is fronted to /ɛ/. Occasionally the glide remains, as in one pronunciation, [brɛɪš], but the responsible glide may not be present. The pronunciation of *judge* as [jɛj], which does not occur in Terre Haute, may reflect the same glide. The presence of /ɛ/ in South Midland pronunciations of *shut, touch,* and *other* seems to stem from simple assimilation rather than from an intrusive glide.[10]

/a/

The symbol [ɑ] is used to represent a low-central unround lax vowel /a/ occurring frequently in the dialect in such words as *cot, watch, water,* and *calm.* The rules for the pronunciation of this vowel may be presented informally as follows:

(1) [ɑ] may be fronted in alveolar environments, as in *hod* [hɑɛd] and *car* [k'ɑɚr]. In the speech of a small minority of informants, [ɑ] may be strongly fronted.

(2) [ɑ] may be retracted in labial and velar (grave) environments to [ɑɛ] or [ɒ], as in *mob* [mɑɹb], *rock* [rɒɹk], *farm* [fɑɹ-ərm], and *far* [fɒər]. It is interesting to note that the retracted or slightly rounded versions do not occur before /r/ in the speech of any of the college-educated informants. On the other hand, the fronted versions of /a/ are not limited to this group.

(3) [ɑ] optionally becomes [ɑə] under the conditions previously listed for the ingliding allophones, but simple lengthening occurs more often than in the case of the front vowels.

/ʊ/

The vowel of such words as *book* and *wood* is characteristically slightly fronted in the dialect in general. More noticeably rounded and retracted versions occur in grave environments, i.e., before and after labials and before the velars, including the velar /l/, as in *hoop* [hʊp] and *pull* [p'ʊɫ]. Before [ɫ], lowering and backing toward /o/ may occur.

The slightly fronted [ʊ] may be advanced or centralized in palatal and alveolar environments, as in *your* [j(ʉ*)ər], *sure* [šʉər], and *should* [š(ʉ*)d]. In the same environments, [ɨ*] occurs in some Terre Haute speech, bringing about the assignment of [ɨ*] to the phoneme /ʊ/. An intrusive j glide may occur before /š/ in the pronunciation of *push* [pʊɪš] and *bush* [bʊɪš]. Except for a single instance, this allophone is limited to the speech of Negro informants. [ʊ] is infrequently diphthongized to [ʊə], except before /r/. Before /ɫ/, a lengthened version of [ʊ] is usual.

TENSE VOWELS

/i/

The principal allophone of the vowel of *beat* and *keep* is a slightly diphthongized variant, [ĭi]. It is convenient to outline the rules of /i/ in terms of modifications of this phone.

(1) [ĭi] usually becomes monophthongal [i] initially, and after /p/, /k/, and /h/. This allophone may occur after labial + liquid or velar + liquid clusters, as in *please* [pliz], *clean* [klin], and *cream* [krim].

(2) [ĭi] becomes [ɾ̆i] after the liquids /l/ and /r/ and after non-grave consonants plus liquid clusters, optionally after the resonants /m/, /w/, and /j/.

(3) [ɾ̆i] stemming from above rule is reduced to [i] or [ɪ] before /l/. Thus *real* and *wheel* may be pronounced as [riəɫ] and [hwiʉɫ] or as [rɪəɫ] and [hwɪɫ]. *He'll* and *she'll* are often pronounced with the lax diphthong.

(4) [ĭi] in any segmental environment optionally, if not generally, is reduced to [i] under level pitch.

* Preferred phonetic symbol not available.

/e/

The rules for the pronunciation of the vowel of *bait* correspond closely with those for /i/. Thus the principal allophone [eˇi] or [ɛˆɪˆ] becomes [eeˆ] where [iˇi] becomes [i], and [eˇi] or [ɛˆɪˆ] becomes [ɛɪ] where [iˇi] becomes [ɪˇi]. Some triphthongs do occur before [ɫ], as in *mail man,* but the middle element can sometimes be caught only when the recording tape is played backwards. As in the case of [iˇi], [eˇi] in any segmental environment tends to reduce to a monophthong or near-monophthong under level pitch.[11]

/ɔ/

The usual vowel of such words as *caught* and *cough* is [ɔˇ], a very open lower mid-back vowel. The typical version of /ɔ/ shades into /ɒ/, a low-back round vowel, in the speech of most informants, especially in alveolar and palatal environments. In the speech of informants who alternate [ɔˇ] and [ɒ], a fairly well rounded [ɔ] occurs before /r/, and raising to [oˇ] is not uncommon. Other informants, who reflect South Midland influences, may evidence some neutralization of /ɑ/, /ɔ/ before /r/, as in pronunciations of *farm* as [fɒərm] and *far* as [fɒər]. Where the onset begins at [ɔˇ] or [ɒ], progressive rounding may occur, especially before the velars /k/, /g/, and /ŋ/, and before /l/. This allophone is rare except in Negro speech and in West Terre Haute speech. It usually occurs under changing pitch. Also occurring under changing pitch is an ingliding allophone. While it may occur in nearly all environments, it is far less common before /k/, /g/, /ŋ/, and /l/ than is a lengthened [ɔˇ]. Finally, an intrusive palatal glide occurs optionally in the dialect before /š/, as in *caution* [k'ɔiˇš(ɨ*)n] and *wash* [w'ɔˇɪš]. This allophone is assigned to /ɔi/.

/o/

The most common realization of the vowel of *boat* and

* Preferred phonetic symbol not available.

home is [oʊ], an upgliding diphthong beginning in a rather close mid-back position and gliding very quickly to a position somewhat dependent on the next phone. Close onsets are customary initially and after labials, velars, and /h/, as in *posts* [pˌoʊs], *coat* [kˌoʊt], and *home* [hoũm]. Fronted versions occur optionally in other environments, as in *drove* [droœʊv]. Unfronted versions tend to reduce to monophthongs under level pitch, especially before /l/ and /r/. Under changing pitch, an ingliding version, [oə], is virtually regular before /r/, as in *weatherboard* [boərd]; and also occurs in some pronunciations of *known* [noən]. Among members of all three generations of Terre Haute informants, the contrast between /o/ and /ɔ/ may be lost, with /o/ more often than not the survivor.

/u/

The variant of the vowel of *boot* occurring most frequently in the dialect is a monophthong [u], often slightly diphthongized to [uˇu]. The monophthong or near monophthong is virtually regular initially and after /h/ and predominates in labial and velar environments, as in *whose spoon* [huz spuˇun] and *coop* [k'up]. [ʊu], a clearly diphthongal variant with a relatively lax onset, occurs occasionally in labial and velar environments and alternates more or less freely with the monophthong after alveolars, affricates, and palatals. In the latter environments fronting to [(ʉ*)u] occurs frequently, and a sharply fronted variant occurring in the same environments seems to be limited almost entirely to the middle generation of women informants. Under level pitch, the monophthong occurs almost uniformly in labial and velar environments.

An examination of the rules for the more tense manifestations of /i/, /e/, /o/, and /u/ permits the general observa-

* Preferred phonetic symbol not available.

tion that monophthongal allophones of these vowels are most likely to occur, in descending order of frequency, (1) in grave environments under level pitch; (2) in grave environments under changing pitch, and (3) in other environments under level pitch.[12]

/ai/

The usual pronunciation of the vowel of *bite* is [ɑɪ˄], a diphthong beginning at the low-central position of the vowel of *father* and ending at a high or high-mid front position. Using the principal variant as a base, the rules for the pronunciation of this diphthong may be stated as follows: The onset of [ɑɪ˄] is optionally slightly fronted to [ɑ˖], as in the word *lines* [lɑ˖ɪnz]. The frequency of occurrence of fronting varies from zero to more than sixty per cent, the latter in Negro speech. The onset may be strongly fronted before /l/ and /r/, primarily but not exclusively in Negro speech, as in some pronunciations of *ironing* [á˖ɪrnɪŋ] and *file* [fa˖ɪɬ]. Before these liquids, the palatal glide may be lost, as in the pronunciation of *file* as [faɬ] and *fire* as [far]. Under change of pitch a schwa may intrude, resulting in the pronunciation of these words as [faəɬ] and [faər]. In the speech of other informants, [ɑɪ] may reduce to [ɑ] before /l/, as in *I'll* [ɑɬ]; and before /r/ in a number of forms, including *wire, fire, tire,* and so on. The latter pronunciations are much more restricted socially than is the pronunciation of *I'll* as [ɑɬ], which is likely to occur under tertiary stress among a wide range of informants. Finally, the onset of [ɑɪ] is sporadically raised toward [ʌ], as in a fairly common pronunciation of *nice* as [nɑ˄ïˇs].

/æu/

The principal variant of the vowel of such words as *town* and *house,* based on its frequency of occurrence and widespread distribution, is [æ˞ʊ], the beginning of which is a lowered and retracted [æ] and the offglide of which is usually quick and lax. The onset, which is rarely an unmodified [æ], is optionally lowered and retracted to [a] in folk and cultivated speech, infrequently so in common speech. Further backing and lowering of the onset to the [ɑ] of *father* occurs in some twenty per cent of the pronunciations of /aeu/ in cultivated speech, in about ten per cent of the pronunciations of the vowel in folk speech, and in no pronunciation of /æu/ in common speech.[13]

/ɔi/

The onset of the vowel of *joint* and *boil,* usually a not very tense [ɔ], may be fronted initially or in alveolar and palatal environments, as in *oysters* [ɔ˞ˇistɚz] and *enjoyed* [ɪnjɔ'c̆ɪ̂d]. Closer onsets are more common, and raising and rounding to [o] occurs after labials in the speech of informants from the three basic *Atlas* categories. Before /l/ the palatal glide is sometimes considerably less prominent and in some older speech may reach no higher than a tense [ɛ]. More often, words with following /l/ are pronounced with three quite distinct elements in the vowel, as in *spoiled* [sp'ɔɪ̂ɛɫd] and *oil* [ɔɪɫl].

THE UNSTRESSED VOWELS

/ə/

In his significant discussion of the Atlanta dialect, James Sledd makes the suggestion "that the most striking phonetic peculiarities of this kind of Atlanta talk . . . can actually be traced to two very simple causes: first, the dialect has two reduction vowels, not just one; and second, two corresponding kinds of glide appear between its consonants and liquids and the syllabics that precede these."[14] Evidence for the presence of two reduced or unstressed vowels is of two related sorts: (1) an intrusive palatal glide to match unstressed [ɪ] and an intrusive velar glide to match unstressed [ə]; and (2) a sizeable corpus of minimal pairs of words contrasting [ɪ] and [ə]. As outlined in the discussion of the stressed vowels, the speech of Terre Haute has both palatal and velar intruding glides. Does it also have two reduction vowels?

If one extrapolates from the limited *Atlas* data the likely Terre Haute pronunciations of minimal pairs cited by Sledd, he finds few contrasts. No contrasts of [ə] and [ɪ] are at all likely in the pronunciation of such pairs as *chorus:iris, crocus:heiress, robot:cubit, mammoth:stinketh, Phillip: tulip, seraph:sheriff,* and *forehead:torrid,* all listed as succesful minimal pairs in the southern states.[15] In the pronunciation of all these forms, the unstressed vowel will be either the mid-central [ə] or a retracted lower high-central [ɨ*], perhaps not improperly symbolized as [ʉ*]. Except for the predominance of [ʉ*] before [ɫ] and the prevalence of [ɨ*] and [ɪ] before the affricates, where in such words as *damage* and *luggage* /e/ or /i/ may also occur, the principal allophones of /ə/ appear to alternate freely in the dialect as a whole. As noted in the Terre Haute study, the occurrence of unstressed [ɪ], with few exceptions, is ascribable to assimilation to an adjacent stressed /ɪ/ or to an adjacent palatal glide. The *Atlas* record of an elderly Negro native of Terre Haute provides most of the exceptions. Interestingly, it is in her speech that one finds the palatalized /r/ so vital to Sledd's hypothesis. Also evident is the vocalization of the palatalized /r/, a feature that Sledd lists as a probable option in current Atlanta speech. Thus one finds in the record of this informant the pronunciation of *large* as [lɑrʲj], [lɒɚɪj], and [lɑːɪj]; *horse* as [hɔɪs], *porch* as [pˌorjč], and *or-*

* Preferred phonetic symbol not available.

anges as [ɔ'rʲɪnj(ɪ*)z] and [áˆɪnjɨz]. The palatalization and vocalization do not affect [ɚ] forms such as *earth* and *worms*. The corollary palatalized or light /l/ occurs in the same informant's speech, as in one pronunciation of *stallion* [st'ælʲjɨn]. In older white speech, in contrast, a velar /l/ with palatal coarticulation occurs in the pronunciation of this word.

Deep Phonology

Although it is of some significance that the preceding discussion lends support to Sledd's hypothesis linking two reduced vowels with two intrusive glides and two versions of both /l/ and /r/, what is more pertinent to the focus of this conference is the fact that such seemingly aberrant versions of /l/ and /r/ apparently are intimately connected with the deep phonology of an idiolect, or, in the case of the southern United States, of a dialect spoken by millions. Nor are such ostensibly negligible aberrations limited in Terre Haute to /l/ and /r/ and the speech of Negro informants. The palatalized versions of /g/, /ŋ/, /š/, and /ž/ mentioned earlier are closely connected with an intrusive palatal glide, with the upgliding allophones of the lax vowels, and apparently with the neutralization of the tense-lax contrast among the front vowels in some idiolects. These observations alone give one hope that a better understanding of the deep phonology of American speech will contribute substantially to the establishment of the relationship between dialects and clinically significant speech problems.

---

* Preferred phonetic symbol not available.

2. NOTES ON A PHILOSOPHY OF
DISORDERED COMMUNICATION:
LANGUAGE ASPECTS

Fred M. Chreist

INTRODUCTION

The teacher or clinician who is assigned the task of training students in the fields of speech and language pathology assumes certain responsibilities. Among the obligations incumbent upon the instructor are demands that he introduce his students to the breadth as well as the limitations of the area of study called speech pathology; that he assist his students in reading and analyzing the applicable research in the various facets of this specialization; and that he be prepared to suggest methods of applying the research findings to the needs of children and adults in the clinic or classroom.

In completing these three major tasks within the framework of the university academic community, it becomes necessary for the instructor or clinical director to develop a philosophy upon which or into which the talents of his individual students can be made applicable to the future life and professional work of each clinician. Such a philosophy, appropriate for language disorders, is needed especially in a country or part of the country where language interference is a daily experience in the lives of many students. Such a setting is that in which the writer has spent the last twenty-one years of his teaching career. It is a setting in which three or more languages overlap; and, as a consequence, frequent interference is discovered in the language function of the student or client in the clinic. In the Southwest, the speaker of English, the speaker of Spanish, and the speaker of one of four or five dialects of an American Indian language are constantly in communication. A philosophy of disordered communication must prepare the student to work with facets of dialectology as they appear in the bilingual, the polyglot,* and the individual having a pathological speech and language problem.

NEED FOR A PHILOSOPHY OF DISORDERED COMMUNICATION

A review of the literature in the field revealed that twenty years ago Kenneth Scott Wood stated his philosophy of "speech correction" with the following introduction:

> The speech correctionist, if he is to be effective, progressive and whole-hearted, must have a working philosophy consisting of something more than the emotionally satisfying reactions which come from helping the handicapped. . . . Early in his training, the student clinician needs to develop a rational philosophy about speech correction which will give him an over-all sense of direction, relationship and purpose. Without such an underpinning in his profession, he may suddenly find himself operating in isolation with the speech mechanism, with speech sounds, and even with the individual. Because he does not have a broad enough concept of what he is doing, he will eventually find himself operating in a vacuum where life seems very dull. . . . In any

* "polyglot" is here used to indicate the individual who has a "confusion of languages."

field of study or profession one cannot remain healthy unless he has a philosophy of justification for his pursuit and unless he can see where it fits in the great jig-saw puzzle . . .
(Wood, 1947)

Since Wood published his philosophy, the field he refers to as "speech correction" has been divided into speech pathology and audiology. These two major areas, in turn, expanded until they include "language pathology" and "education of the deaf" as major concerns of the student and the clinician. Mary E. Switzer underlined the crux of this change in direction: "In this approach to an understanding of ourselves, we are, admittedly on the perimeter. But two great steps forward have been taken; we have begun to grasp the fundamental importance of communication as a researchable entity, and we have recognized that speech and hearing problems occupy as crucial a position in our total research as any other functional pathologies" (Switzer, 1959). We have moved from "speech correctionists" to "speech pathologists and audiologists" interested in language structure and function as a constantly operating part of the communication process.

In the late 1950s and the early 1960s, the findings of linguists were being utilized by speech pathologists, particularly in the study of language development and aphasia in children and in adults. The need for a better understanding of the language function as a developmental factor in speech acquisition and loss through trauma or progressive disintegration became evident in speech pathology and audiology. As an academic discipline, speech has always utilized the research findings of other sciences; perhaps we have been too dependent upon research and clinical workers trained in other fields of study. Whatever may be the feelings of this group on the matter, it is evident that the contributions from students of linguistics are essential to an understanding of the development of speech and hearing in the child and the problem of individuals who suffer from pathological language involvement. It is also evident from the statements of Wood (1947), Switzer (1959), and Siegel (1967).

When explaining the structure of his research, Siegel states: "The experiments summarized in this paper evolved within an interpersonal framework. Briefly, this framework suggests that whenever A and B are together in a social situation, the behavior of each is at least partially a function of the responses and characteristics of the other. This approach seems especially cogent in the study of communication disorders since speech events are almost always interpersonal, involving both a speaker and a listener. Even if A is a speech clinician and B a child coming for correction, not only does the clinician modify the behavior of the child but the child exerts some influence over the behavior of the clinician" (Siegel, 1967).

A restatement of a philosophy of speech pathology and audiology is needed. Such a statement should expand the philosophy of speech correction presented by Wood to include consideration for relevant developments in the areas of audiology, teaching of the deaf, and language disordered communication. It is the purpose of this paper to make some notes on the language aspects of the philosophy after attempting to establish a working definition of disordered communication.

BASIS OF THE PHILOSOPHY: THE PERSON

A philosophy of disordered human communication must have as its basis the client, as a person. "Any philosophy that pretends to some relevance to human experience, its description, or evaluation, must at some time come to grips with the question of what man is and to what purpose, if any, he exists. Upon our concept of person and what it means to be human, there depend not only matters of practical concern such as the conduct of our lives and our behavior towards other people but also matters of theoretical concern as is obviously the case with the human sciences" (O'Malley, 1966).

Note two statements from the paragraph above that will have significance for our discussion of disordered language and communication. First, the "matters of practical concern" associated with the concept of person are of importance to our discussion of dialectology, for it is in the "conduct of our lives" and "our behavior towards other people" that we become intensely involved with our students and clients who speak a language other than English. Second, the "matters of theoretical concern" are vital for our discussion of a philosophy of disordered language in communication because speech pathology and audiology are members of the field of human sciences, and the foundations of experimental research in the laboratory or in the clinic are theoretical postulates concerning the bases of disordered language behavior.

The speech pathologist is "utterly dependent upon a thorough understanding of speech itself as a form of human behavior," to quote Wood (1947). "To comprehend the speech act we must understand the person himself. Conversely, no person can really be understood apart from his speech. . . . Every syllable uttered is in some way a reflection of the personality of the person who utters it."

Language and human individuality are inexorably tied together. Our concept of person and what it means to be human will influence the type of philosophy structures for use in the profession of speech pathology. The speech and language function will be discussed on the basis of a bipolar approach. From one point of view man must be regarded as an animal with a thoroughly biological basis of speech (Lenneberg, 1967). Behavior is in general a part of our animal constitution, and "the characteristics of species specificity and plasticity inherent in behavior are particularly relevant to investigations of speech and language because, on the one hand, this behavior is specific to the species *Homo sapiens,* and on the other hand, there is an obvious degree of plasticity that accounts for divergence between modern natural languages."

In this regard, man could be considered an animal, capable of being conditioned, trained, or "educated" to acquire and use any language which the experimenter or the clinician desired. An element of the conditioned approach is evident in human language learning; modern research verifies its presence, and the success of machine programs and patterned practice language drills support the conclusion. But the "machine is not enough." Even the theorists who maintain a strict biological approach to language concede that other factors are relevant. These other factors provide the second point for our bipolar approach to language learning and relearning, *concept formation* and *utilization,* what Noam Chomsky has called "linguistic competence" (Chomsky, 1967).

The contributions of concept formation and use are essential to the student or client who would learn English as a nonnative language. Our discussion of dialectology must include the consideration of depth understanding in speech communication if we hope to attain even partial success with the students learning English as a second language. The same may be said for the client who comes to our clinic handicapped by lack of language foundations or an overlap of languages that causes interference. This facet of language study is related to the philosophy of disordered communication in the way that Gabriel Marcel's concept of "having" and "being" finds expression (Marcel, 1952) : "in order to *have* effectively it is necessary to *be* in some degree, that is to say, in this case, to be immediately for one's self, to feel one's self, as it were affected or modified."

A poignant manner of stating the bipolar approach to the language function is presented in a description of the method used by Henry James in building his literary works, "both from the outside in (that is, in accordance with some predetermined ideas of what the shape should be) and from the inside out (that is, in accordance with the organic development of the 'germ') " (Ward, 1967).

COMMUNICATION: NORMAL AND DISORDERED

Communication has been defined in so many different ways and for so many purposes that it seems redundant to add another definition to the already overburdened collection. More appropriate would be the choice of one of the already stated definitions, if it were not the feeling of the writer that the multitude of definitions reviewed lack one or more of the aspects of a definition needed in the fields of speech pathology and audiology. If a basic philosophy of disordered communication in the most complete terms, applicable to dialectology as well as to the variety of disorders of speech and hearing we see in the clinic, is eventually to be formulated, then all elements in the communication process must be included. Let us state our operational definition in terms broad enough to include the many aspects of the genetic contribution to human behavior and to the forms of breakdown in the language function. Such a definition should be specific enough to include a consideration of patterns of information acquisition and transfer by the human organism, as well as to explain the utilization of such information in terms of the influence of environmental stimulation that encourages language development and use. Finally, the definition should include those factors usually assigned to speech and hearing, the production and transfer of ideas used in the daily life of the communicator.

In terms of these requirements we have defined communication as *a process of transferring materials, information, and ideas from a producer or source, to a receiver or destination, utilizing a transmission chain or medium.* Feedback is a necessary part of such a process in human speech and language learning.

Reduction of efficiency of the human communication system may come from a variety of sources or causes. In terms of speech production and reception, this reduction in efficiency can occur in the producing mechanism, the encoding and transmitting mechanisms, or the receiving and interpreting mechanisms. When such reduction in efficiency occurs, the entire communication process is influenced. "Noise" has been used by specialists in information theory and the mathematical theory of communication to denote "changes in transmitted signals" (Shannon and Weaver, 1964). This basic word in the vocabulary of the communication engineer as well as the layman speaking of communication has been used in this paper as a generic term meaning "reduction in efficiency of the communication system." Thus, we will speak of "physical noise," "semantic noise," and, of most significance to us in this discussion, "linguistic noise." Noise of any type disrupts the communication process by reducing its efficiency; this frequently results in a referral of the communicator to the speech and hearing specialist for remedial assistance (Chreist, 1964).

Reception. Remedial assistance may take one of several forms. The client may need reconstruction of his receptive and interpretive mechanisms. Modern means of accomplishing this are provided by surgical intervention, by prosthetic substitution or addition, or through the use of a subsidiary communication channel in order to direct information into the final integrating center. Examples of these three methods suggested above are the tympanoplasty or myringoplasty or fenestration operation used for reconstruction of the physical communication system; the hearing aid or amplifying system for prosthetic assistance, and the use of speech reading for the individual having an acoustic handicap severe enough to make it impossible for the client to use the normal auditory channel. Assistance at the peripheral level of involvement, although crude in its present form, has been advancing steadily because of the contributions of our technologists and research oriented scientists. Unfortunately, the need for understanding the interpreting and coordinating functions of the human language system is still to be satisfied. It is to discuss possible approaches to an understanding of this function that this conference has been called.

Production. The client may need assistance in the production and transmission phases of speech and language. In the case of either production or transmission, the speech clinician or teacher has frequently been inclined to work on the symptom with little regard for the native language sound components, structure, or semantic content. Therapists working with individuals speaking two or more languages have frequently been confused by the acoustic and behavior symptoms presented by the client who is "polyglot" or demonstrates evidence of language interference.

The oral symptom or observed behavioral pattern is important in diagnosing and evaluating the problems of dialectology, but the use of this observational data alone for remedial purposes could lead to a superficial treatment of a "deep" involvement in speech and language (Corder, 1966; MacDonald, 1964).

Concept formation. When the "deep" aspects of the language function are studied, it becomes evident that cognition and concept formation are essential parts of such a structure. Cognition will be used in terms of Guilford's definition of the word: "cognition means discovery, rediscovery or recognition" (Guilford, 1959). For purposes of clinical work with clients having language disorders and language interference, the writer has found the Farradane model of concept formation useful. This model is reproduced in figure 1. The Farradane theory says: "In general terms, two main types of mental processes seemed to be demonstrable, that of increasing *memory* or sense of mental time, and that of increasing *concept clarity*" (Farradane, 1963).

FIGURE 1

Mental Time or Memory ⟶

	Non-time	Temporary	Fixed	
Concurrent	Concurrence	Self-Activity Comparison	Association	Conceptual clarity
Non-distinct	Equivalence	Dimensional State	Appurtenance	
Distinct	Distinctness	Reaction	Causation or Functional Dependence	↓

If we conceive of learning as the process of concept formation and use the Webster definition of concept as "a mental image of a thing formed by generalization from particulars," then concept formation could be "acquiring or utilizing a common response to dissimilar stimuli." On the basis of such an assumption we would have described language learning in terms of the Farradane model of concept formation. Projecting the "concept" into the Guilford model, *Structure of the Intellect* (Guilford, 1959), as suggested by Farradane, we can place a single concept in the "Product" dimension of the model under what Guilford designates as a *unit* of the product series; units, classes, relations, systems, transformations, and implications. Using such an assumption, concepts become a part of the "deep" structure of language learning or relearning.

Language learning, in terms of the model, would include at the first or "concurrent" level, the acquisition of those parts of language taught by classical, instrumental, or operant *conditioning*. We will call the second plane, designated by Farradane the "non-distinct" stage, the *mechanical structuring* level of concept formation. Since the third or highest level of concept clarity includes cultural and psychological attachments that appear to be acquired only through association and long practice, we shall call this level the *emotional attachment* level in language concept formation. At this level the concept becomes distinctive, according to Farradane.

An experiment can be structured on the verbal expression of concepts found among children. A list of five questions is prepared, each asking for a response to the questions asked. Instructions allow the child to guess if he does not know the answer; he may also answer "I do not know" if he prefers. The questions are, What is a "dog"? What is a "shmoo"?

What is an "ugab"? What is a "batman"? What is a "____"?
(from Dr. Seuss). Questions are randomly arranged and
asked of a selected group of children of the same age level
and varying cultural backgrounds. It is postulated that the
response of the children will give evidence of various levels
of expressed concept development and that cultural and language background will influence these responses. "Ugab" is
the only nonsense word.

The child learning English as a native language is conditioned at the first level to respond to his pet dog, Rex, with
the name "dog," "doggie," or "goggie," depending on how
thoroughly the process has been completed at this level. He
is taken for a ride in the country and sees a horse in a distant
field. Responding to the stimulus the child says, "dog." Our
subject, not having learned the mechanical relationships of
distance orientation, may generalize from the "fixed" association made at the concurrent level, causing confusion by
failure to recognize the equivalence caused by distance.

This same condition occurs constantly in working with
the student learning English as a second language. Thoroughly conditioned to his native language in depth, and
superficially conditioned to English, he fails to recognize,
receptively, the phonemes of American English that serve as
allophones in his native language. The discrimination experiments discussed in the second part of this paper will
illustrate this assumption. Learning the mechanical features
of the language in terms of individual sound components,
structure, syntax, and semantics will enable the student to
respond more efficiently in the receptive and interpretive
features of the language. It will also be one step in assisting
him in production of these mechanical features.

In terms of the Farradane model, the student will need to
learn the features of equivalence causing the interference,

give the new sound or structure a "dimensional" state in his language usage, and learn the appurtenances that go with the structure of the new language. An example of such an appurtenance characteristic of structure that causes trouble for the student is the modifier patterns in two languages. Differences and similarities in the placement of modifying words differ in such languages as English and Chinese (Yao Shen, 1966). A similar difficulty occurs at the mechanical level in Spanish and Portuguese. The native speakers of Spanish and Portuguese are inclined to add the word *to* after *must* in such patterns as "I must go to the student union." The student learning English as a second language will often say, "I must to go to the student union." Lado points out that this frequently heard addition "results from the student's native language habit of using que in a similar pattern (Spanish, "Tengo que ir"; Portuguese, "Eu tenho que ir")." An English pattern having *to* in the same position— "I have to go to the library"—reinforces the tendency (Lado, 1966). Native language habits at the mechanical structural level will interfere with the learning of American English or any other second language because of certain differences in the mechanical uses of modifying words, to use only one of innumerable illustrations available.

Let us return to the child acquiring the concept of the word "dog"; if we take the child to the side of the horse, the distance equivalence tends to disappear. Sensory information acquired by the child in association with dogs and horses, whether acquired by touch, sight, audition, or any of the other sensory avenues will help to clarify the concept in terms of dimensional state and appurtenances. The child soon learns that the horse has a tail and surface covering that differs from the dog. He may also have different external appendages, indicating by these whether the four-legged animal is a mare, a stallion, or a gelding. These, then, are mechanical features of concept formations and are a necessary part of the concept formation process of the child or the student learning a second language.

One of the necessary beginning points in language work with emotionally or neurologically involved children, as well as with the culturally deprived child, is the teaching of the "self concept," beginning with the mechanical features of the body itself and working in the differentiation between the name of the child and the use of the phrase, "I am _____" (May, 1968).

When we enter the third level of concept clarity, the emotional features contribute to concept clarity. Every language has deep cultural and emotional associations. Depth of concept is associated with the distinctiveness in the Farradane model as adapted for use in language pathology and dialectology.

The child's dog, Rex, or whatever he has chosen to call him, is distinctive; he has acquired this distinctiveness because of the child's constant association with him in various life settings. The same must be said of the native language; we have grown up with it, loved it (or hated it, depending on the cultural and emotional attitudes taken by those close to us), suffered with it, prayed with it, and bargained with it.

At this level the individual with second language problems may encounter negative emotional characteristics of social or political significance. History verifies the existence of this type of emotional conflict as well as intellectual handicap in Wales, Puerto Rico, and the American Southwest (Tireman, 1948).

Problems of language concept acquisition experienced at this level may be illustrated from experiences of students with the word "father" in two cultures, Zuñi and American English family life. "To the Zuñi child, the word father will suggest the father in a consanguinal relationship, the basic ties are those of 'blood,' while in a conjugal relationship the basic tie is the love relationship." (Zintz, 1963) For all facets of the word "father" there will be a contrast in the cultural and emotional relationship between the Zuñi word and the American English word. It is possible to say that at the third or *distinct* level of Farradane's model, emotional and cultural factors become so important that the majority of second language students never assimilate these features for more than their native language.

Rex, at this level, is different from all other dogs, even if they are exactly the same breed, have the same markings and coloring, and might be easily confused by the unassociated observer. For the child, Rex always reacts with attention and love when you pull his tail, but another dog may bite in the identical situation. Thus *reaction* becomes part of the depth associations with a concept.

The child's concept of Rex at the functional dependence level could be expressed in terms of the fact Rex will lick your face and attempt to distract you when he sees that you are crying or despondent. He is always ready to romp and play when you want him to share your enthusiasm or fun. These represent the emotional ties developed by the child for "My dog, Rex." It is at this level of concept formation that the semantic, emotional, and cultural factors associated with the word, sentence, or situation help to clarify the concept.

When the client or the student with a foreign accent comes for remedial assistance, this "distinct" or deep level of concept is the most difficult for you as a clinician to impart. Techniques of instruction need to be made available to the student clinician and teacher for working with students at this level. The Farradane model has been used for explanation of concept development because it seems to be the most lucid presentation of the steps through which the clinician or teacher must go in order to understand the development of a native language and to understand the points of interference encountered by students learning English as a second language.

This section of a philosophy of disordered communication has attempted to underline the significance of concept formation (Amster, 1966; Bourne, 1966; Clausmeier and Harris, 1966) in the processes of reception and production of speech and language. It is not the purpose of the paper to discuss the detailed relationships that are present in the individual for perception and synthesis as parts of the speech and language process, as such matters have had coverage in recently published books (Bosma, 1967; Flanagan, 1965; Gibson, 1966; and Lieberman, 1967). Neither has it been the intention to present a detailed discussion of the learning process as it relates to dialectology, since this material may be found in such publications as Lin, 1965; Engel et al., 1966; and Johnson and Myklebust, 1967.

If the presentation seems oversimplified, it is only because the writer, as an instructor and educator of clinicians in the area of double language pathology, has found it necessary to explain, in these terms, what appears to be one of the fundamental building blocks in language learning. In the literature, the constant use of the terms "concept" and "conceptualization" as abstractions has confused the student, clinician, and teacher. It is in an attempt to clarify the use of the term in relation to language learning that the research on this subject was initiated.

Let us summarize our statements on a philosophy of disordered communication as they apply to *Communicology* and *Dialectology*.

SUMMARY OF NOTES ON LANGUAGE ACQUISITION

If we begin with a statement presented earlier, "a philosophy of disordered human communication must have as its basis the client as a person," we can make the following assertions about this communicating person:

(1) The human individual is a *living animal* and, therefore, is constantly in a state of change while seeking to maintain a stable state, homeostasis, according to the biologists.

(2) *Reproduction* is the fundamental process of the living state (Mercer, 1962). Such a condition exists at the cellular level as well as the level of the individual human animal. Reproduction takes place among humans through the transfer of materials, the sperm cell of the male invading the ovum cell of the female. Thus, reproduction, the life creating act in communication, results from transfer of materials.

(3) For the speech pathologist and audiologist, the significance of this life creating communication event is the *transmission of genetic properties.* In the 1940s it became increasingly apparent that a chemical compound of chromosomes, deoxyribonucleic acid (DNA), is the essential substance of inheritance, or reproduction, and also important for controlling the life of the cell (Mercer, 1962). A second ribonucleic acid (RNA) was later found to be present in the cytoplasm of the cell and to cooperate with DNA in laying down the patterns of genetic characteristics of the embryo.

(4) It is agreed by most authorities that structural *form,* at least in part, determines *function.* The human acquires language because his anatomical, physiological, and neuro-

logical systems make symbolic recognition and production possible.

(5) The sensory neural system of man is so structured that information may be obtained and transferred from the outside world or the internal environment or the body to the central integrating organ. *Information transfer* of this type is essential to concept formation and learning.

(6) Ideas are based on concepts *conditioned* at the most superficial level; strengthened at a *mechanical usage* level where structural form, syntactical relationships, and semantic associations are inserted into the pattern; and, finally, *emotionally strengthened* at the "deep" level of associated *cultural experience.*

(7) Language and speech are essential to the structure of the intellect. The *concept* has been presented as a "unit" of this structure. A complex model such as the "structure of the intellect" hypothesized by Guilford and supported by experimental evidence, necessarily describes a multidimensional functioning process or group of processes.

(8) Disordered communication may have a variety of causes, genetically or environmentally engendered. Among those problems found in the clinic of the classroom is *language interference* caused by the intrusion of native language habits and concepts on the learning and use of a second language.

(9) *Dialectology,* as a study of language and speech differences found in areas where language interference is present, should provide basic directions for expanded research in the laboratory, the clinic, and the classroom.

(10) *Clinical* and *educational techniques* based on the research findings in speech pathology, audiology, linguistics, psychology, and dialectology should provide for work with disordered communication caused by "linguistic noise."

3. SEGMENTING THE STREAM OF SPEECH

James F. Curtis

I feel compelled to begin by making an explicit and unequivocal disclaimer of any expertise in the area of dialectology. Anyone who has read a standard textbook or two on the phonetics of American English and who has browsed a bit through such publications as *American Speech, Language,* etc., knows as much if not more than I concerning dialects, how they develop, and what, if anything, ought to be done about them.

Any hope that I may have of making a contribution to this conference on dialectology arises from the fact that I spend some part of my time (when I am not trying to make like an administrator) in teaching in the rather loosely defined area that is sometimes connoted by the term *experimental phonetics* and in trying to squeeze in a bit of time for research, also in that area. We need not here concern ourselves with an exact definition of experimental phonetics. The important point is that people with interests in this area are involved with the analysis of speech signals, sometimes from an acoustical point of view, sometimes from an interest in the physiological events of speech-sound generation, sometimes in order to learn more about the processes of speech perception. It may also be germane that the work I have been doing for a considerable number of years is carried on in the context of a department that has a substantial concern with *disorders* of the communicative processes. In this context it is natural, I think, that one may have a special reason to consider the research issues and problems of physiological phonetics, acoustic phonetics, speech perception, etc., in relation to the problems of individual behavior and behavior modification.

Persons who spend any significant part of their time attempting to observe and describe speech analytically must inevitably become involved with the problem of segmentation of the more-or-less continuous time series that we call speech. Running speech simply can not be meaningfully observed, analyzed, and measured in its totality. If, for example, one tries to study relationships between the acoustical wave forms that constitute the speech signal and the chain of physiological events that produces the signal one must deal with units of some kind. It may be obvious, but I don't think that it is always clearly recognized, that the decision concerning the unit of analysis to be employed is of the most basic importance. It does make a significant difference how one segments the stream of speech. The particular choice that is made will have an inevitable effect on the nature of relationships that we deduce, the classification systems that we may develop, the types of measurement that we consider to be relevant, and the fundamental nature of the models that we may invent in our attempts to explain basic physical, physiological, and psychological processes.

For most of us any suggestion of segmenting the stream of speech into units immediately suggests the process of making a phonetic (or phonemic) transcription of an utterance.

This is natural enough since most of us received our first real experience with observing speech analytically, and attempting to describe it with some degree of precision, when we learned to record the speech we hear by employing a conventional system of phonetic or phonemic symbols. Thus we learned to segment speech into phone-size units. If we continued to study and work with speech, as linguists, phoneticians, speech pathologists, etc., we doubtless have practiced this type of auditory analysis and description until we have become highly skilled at it. However unnatural and forced such an analysis may have seemed at the beginning, as practice continued it doubtless came to seem more and more natural. The phone-size segments (speech sounds, phonemes, etc.) that are assigned separate symbols in the transcription process also may have come to be regarded as the natural units of speech analysis, so much so, in fact, that it would be quite unlikely to occur to most of us that any other segmentation of the speech stream would be possible. In short, most of us have come to accept as axiomatic the fundamental assumption that the speech stream is, in point of fact, a linear sequence of discrete units each of which can be labeled and classified, and which can be considered to be independent and commutable. Moreover, not only has it apparently not occurred to many persons to question this assumption, but, further, it has been little realized that the validity of this assumption may be related to the particular purpose for which speech is being analytically studied; that is, whether one's primary concern is with the description of linguistic structure, the analysis of speech production, the psychoacoustical relationships of speech perception, the acquisition of language by small children, or the learning of a foreign language by an adult. The same segmentation is commonly assumed to be appropriate for all such purposes.

My fundamental purpose in these remarks, and I hope it is consistent with the purposes of this conference, is to raise some questions about the apparently seldom-questioned assumption that the only correct way to analyze speech is as a string of speech sounds or phones. I think this is worth doing because it seems to me that some of the data that have been coming from the experimental phonetics laboratories concerning the processes of articulation and speech perception are difficult to reconcile with this assumption.

In the description of language structure a phonology based on the phoneme as the fundamental segment and the assumption that speech can be analyzed as a linear string of phonemes appears to work very well. Morris Halle (1964) in a discussion of the unit for phonological analysis demonstrates neatly and very persuasively that any other assumption simply gets one into trouble, in particular that segmenting into phone-size units makes it possible to state certain relational rules in a relatively simple and straightforward fashion, whereas any other assumption leads to awkwardness and greatly increased complexity. Obviously, for the purposes of phonological analysis and for the purposes of classical phonetics, one can divide speech into phone-size segments. So long as one depends completely on an observer who has *learned* to make this kind of an auditory analysis of speech, no real difficulties are encountered.

However, as soon as one attempts to examine the acoustic wave forms of speech, or some transform of the raw acoustic signal such as a speech spectrogram, he immediately encounters problems. Neither the raw wave form nor any of the transforms that have been developed show natural dividing points corresponding to boundaries between successive phones. Although certain discontinuities are evident in the acoustic signal, these may or may not correspond to divisions between phones. For example, a series of vowels and sonorous consonants, such as nasal or liquids, will show relatively continuous change without such discontinuities. On the other hand, the spectrograms of an utterance containing stops will show discontinuities (for example, between the implosion and explosion phases of the consonants) at locations that would have to be considered to be in the middle of the phone—certainly not at its boundaries. Thus the acoustic record does not provide information that enables one to carry out a segmentation process.

If one examines records of physiological behavior, he will often find himself in an equally difficult position, so far as locating boundaries between time segments corresponding to phone elements is concerned. Throughout much of speech the articulators are in relatively continuous movement, and landmarks for time segments corresponding to phones on tracings that depict jaw movement, tongue movement, air pressure or flow, etc. turn out to be conspicious by their absence in many instances. In point of fact, therefore, it is very difficult to find much verification in either the acoustic or the physiological data for the view that speech may be analyzed as a string of discrete elements.

The problem of defining speech segments by reference to acoustic and physiological data extends beyond the lack of discreteness in such data, however. It is further complicated by the fact that neither acoustic phonetics research nor physiological phonetics research has so far succeeded very well in identifying invariant sets of acoustical or physiological characteristics that show neat one-to-one correspondence to the phonemes which we discriminate with relative ease.

All this is, of course, well known and hypotheses to explain the lack of invariant characteristics corresponding to phonemes have been advanced. The most common explanation is what may be termed the "target hypothesis." Essentially this hypothesis proposes that each distinctive speech sound corresponds to an idealized acoustic pattern, or an idealized articulatory gesture, that may be called a target. An idealized speech utterance is viewed as a linear string of such targets. Such an idealized utterance would presumably be realized if the articulators were free to move at sufficiently rapid rates and were free of all mechanical constraints. In actual speech, however, the idealized targets are seldom realized because (1) the rapidity of movement required for precise execution of targets during running speech is greater than the inertia of the articulators will permit, and (2) the mechanical constraints placed on the movement of articulators due to their anatomical interconnections with other structures sometimes limit their movements. Thus, the idealized patterns are only approximated in actual speech. From an articulatory point of view, the hypothesis suggests that running speech may be viewed as a series of near misses of idealized targets, together with intervening transitional patterns. The corresponding acoustical time series is also a relatively smeared version of idealized phoneme signals interspersed with interphonemic transitional characteristics.

There is, in fact, a good deal of experimental data that may be interpreted as supporting this view, especially for vowels. Beginning with a 1937 study by Black, there has been a series of experiments that includes a 1952 study by Gordon Peterson, a 1961 study by Fairbanks and Grubb, a 1963 study by Stevens and House, and a 1963 study by Lindblom, to name only a selected few, all of which support the concept of an idealized target that is degraded or perturbed, to use the Stevens and House term, as a result of being placed in a context of surrounding phonemes—the amount of perturbation being a predictable function of the speaking rate.

It is also part of this "target hypothesis" that, although the connected speech actualization of the phoneme may become badly smeared in terms of its articulatory movement patterns and the associated acoustic characteristics, there is, at some level in the neuromuscular processing, a distinctive unit corresponding to the phoneme. It has been suggested for example (Cooper, 1966) that the place to look for isomorphic correspondence with phonemes may be at the level of the neural signals that govern the movements of the muscles involved in speech articulation and phonation. In other words, it is suggested that the fundamental view of speech as a linear series of discrete elements would be found to be valid if only one could observe the series of neural signals that control the speech mechanism. The "smearing" that prevents one from confirming this view of speech with data on speech movements and acoustical analysis of utterances is due to the mechanical limitations of the peripheral speech mechanism which assure that articulatory execution will be context-dependent and time-limited. Of course none of this is really new. The basic phenomenon under discussion has long been known to phoneticians who have applied to it the term *assimilation*. The data from laboratory experiments have made it possible to give a somewhat more exact and elegant statement to the manifestations of assimilation, but the basic idea has not thereby been appreciably altered. The point I wish to make is that the phenomenon of assimilation has long been observed and the fundamental ideas of segmentation in phone-size units have nevertheless survived.

However, certain recent studies of articulatory processes have yielded data that are not so readily accounted for by the "target hypothesis." Examples of these studies include the work of Öhmann (1966) at Stockholm on coarticulation, Kozhevnikov and Chistovich, (1965) and Daniloff (1967). The fundamental point is that these studies appear to show a kind of context interaction in the realization of phonemes that cannot be accounted for on the basis of peripheral factors, such as anatomical constraints or mass and inertia of structures. The apparent overlapping among phones which these studies have demonstrated extends over several phone-size segments and the direction of the apparent influence extends both forward and backward. Neither of these facts lends itself to a simple explanation based on such peripheral factors as structural inertia and anatomical constraints. In other words, these interactions must somehow inhere in the neural signals that govern the movements of the peripheral speech mechanism. Thus, the neural signals can no longer be viewed as bearing a one-to-one relation to a linear time series of discrete elements, such as phones or phonemes.

The discussion to this point has been concerned with the problem of segmentation of the speech stream. The usual assumption, often taken for granted rather than explicitly recognized, that speech may be viewed as a linear sequence of phone-size units has been examined. It appears that, while the type of phonological analysis based on that assumption is useful in describing language structure, neither the data from the acoustical analysis of speech signals nor the data concerning the articulatory movements of speech generation show this kind of structure. More recent experimental studies appear to show that even the neural signals that control the speech musculature are not organized as a simple linear sequence of motor commands.

What has all this to do with dialect? Let me see if I can

suggest how I think it may be related. In the first place I would infer that, if one is interested in making a phonological study of a dialect for the purpose of describing its basic structure so that he may compare the structures of two or more dialects, then the procedures of analysis into direct phone-size units assumed to be organized as linear strings would be appropriate. However, if one's purpose is to compare the articulatory movement patterns or the acoustical characteristics of two or more dialects, it would appear that an analysis into phone-size segments would not be very useful.

There are, of course, still other possible goals for dialect study. Some may be very practical goals; for example, assisting a person to change his manner of speaking so as to eliminate certain dialect characteristics that are not completely socially acceptable. Such a concern with dialect is, of course, very nearly parallel to the concern of the speech pathologist for a person whose articulatory patterns are judged to be defective. In either case one is concerned with speech as a motor skill; moreover, this is a motor skill that has become very highly overlearned because of long practice. It is, I believe, fair and reasonable to ask: What are the characteristics of the model of the speech production process that will be most relevant for this kind of interest in speech? When one's purpose is to analyze speech as a type of learned motor behavior, is the appropriate model one that assumes a chain of elemental motor habits that may be regarded as independent and capable of concatenation with relatively few constraints on sequence or order? If such a chain model is assumed, what are the nature and size of the behavioral unit? These questions seem to me to be of fundamental importance if one is going to analyze behavior for the purpose of reaching decisions concerning what behavioral elements within a complex pattern of skilled motor activity may be manipulated, altered, changed, etc.

I do not presume to know the answer to the questions just raised. To the best of my knowledge no experiments have been done that would provide direct evidence for or against such a model or that would cast light on the question of appropriate behavioral units. With very few exceptions the experimental work that has attempted to analyze or manipulate speech behavior has simply borrowed from classical phonetics the model of speech as a linear sequence of discrete phone, or phoneme, size units. The phone has been treated as though it were, in fact, an independent element that could be functionally separated from the stream of speech without causing it to be changed in any radical manner. It appears that investigators, clinicians, and speech teachers have all assumed that the very complex set of motor skills by means of which speech is generated can be validly viewed as a chain of phone-size little habits. As I previously remarked, I do not presume to know enough to propose a model that will accurately represent speech as a type of skilled motor behavior, but I seriously doubt that such a model will be based on behavioral units having the time dimensions of phones. All the evidence that I know about from physiological phonetics seems to me to suggest some other size or type of unit.

Thus, I would like to suggest that, to the extent that our concern with dialect makes us interested in speech viewed as learned motor behavior, we spend some time discussing the possible models that may be thought to represent the known characteristics of the complex of skilled movements required for speech to be generated. Inherent in such a discussion, of course, is a consideration of how such complex behavior may be analyzed into elements or units.

4. BASIC FACTORS RELATING TO DEVELOPMENT OF A DIALECT BY DISADVANTAGED CHILDREN

Charles G. Hurst, Jr.

THE PROBLEM

A basic issue in the area of children's growth and development concerns the effects of early environmental influences on the speech and language (or dialect) patterns that young children, especially the underprivileged, develop.

The overall development of a child may be divided in four parts: physical; personality, including the process of socialization; intellectual; and language, including dialect (or more inclusively, phonology, morphology, and syntax). These four parts intertwine in complex ways to make up the process of human growth (McNeill, 1968). It is clear, for example, that socialization depends on the acquisition of language and that language acquisition depends on socialization; the former is substantiated by the fact that the social conformity is dependent on the linguistic (dialectal) conformity and the latter, at least in part, by the fact that there are linguistic (dialectal) differences among the social classes. Similarly, there are obvious interactions between the acquisition of language and the growth of intellect. Equally important is the connection between all these and the maturational process. Moreover, it is imperative to understand the contribution of environmental influences, including parental awareness and interaction.

A language is acquired through discovering the relations that exist between the surface structure of its sentences and the universal aspects of its deep structure. This phenomenon is partially a manifestation of the child's own (innate) capacities, and partially a representation of the transformations for which the parents and the social subsection serve as models. In an attempt to discover interrelations and ultimate impacts of the multiple variable cited above on the language development of young children, a research program is currently in process at Howard University, Washington, D. C. to study longitudinally the development of language in preschool children from different socioeconomic, cultural, and racial backgrounds. Important to the objectives of this discussion is the knowledge that there are significant differences in speech language patterns which can be observed at an early age and which become more and more apparent along with the maturation. Some of the questions we need to answer through this three-year longitudinal and experimental study of racially and culturally different preschool children are:

(1) What are the crucial aspects of the environment that play a dominant role in shaping dialect during the three-year period beginning with age two?

(2) What are the specific effects on dialect of experiences gained during the period beginning at age two and ending at age five on the acquisition of language?

(3) To what extent is the environment of the three years

immediately preceding the first grade an influencing factor in language competence and performance?

(4) What are the deep and surface structure differences of speech and language acquisition among preschool age children of varying racial and socioeconomic background?

Even the widespread efforts in vogue currently such as Project Headstart to introduce what are referred to as enrichment and remedial programs during early years suffer from a lack of knowledge about the very nature of the dialect problem that exists for so many underprivileged children at the time of entrance to school. In order to help these children, it is important to study information about idiosyncrasies of usage that differentiate language systems; about suprasegmentals such as pitch, stress, and juncture that provide intonational clues to meanings; and about utterance patterns (simple sentence, compound and complex patterns, and ellipses of reduced forms) that can serve as an important index of verbal development. Furthermore, there is also a need to make quantitative studies at various age levels of disadvantaged groups. The acquisition of different grammatical classes befitting to both competence and performance models (Chomsky, 1967), the acquisition of the semantic features, and the distinctive phonological features must be compared.

Based on what we now know, the nonstandard dialect of the poor and underprivileged is characterized by rigidity of syntax and restricted use of verbal organization. It lacks the specificity and exactness needed for precise conceptualization and differentiation. It is a language often used in formal situations where there is a common background of experience. It is characterized by simple, short, and often unfinished sentences, little use of subordinate clauses for elaborating the content of the sentence, restricted use of adverbial and adjectival qualification, lack of continuity and organization of thought, frequent use of categorical statements, and constraint of the self-reference pronouns. It is a language of implicit meaning, commonly shared and easily understood. The formal (or standard) language is one in which the communication is individualized and where the formal possibilities of sentence organization are used to clarify meaning and make it explicit. It is characterized by accurate grammatical order and syntax, complex sentence organization including the use of subordinate clauses, frequent use of prepositions that denote abstract qualities, frequent use of the personal pronoun, and highly individualized qualification. It is a language that emphasizes a complex conceptual hierarchy for organizing experience (Bernstein, 1960).

In a very real sense, therefore, we need to identify both the quantitative and qualitative differences among the language systems and speech behaviors of various socioeconomic and racial groups and to discover the essentials for the development of appropriate and efficacious programs of remediation and enrichment in preschool and elementary school situations.

BACKGROUND

Lenneberg's (1967) model demonstrates that normal children, not impaired by deafness, brain damage, or other physical or psychic disorders, begin to babble at about six months, utter a first "word" at 10 to 12 months, combine words at 18 to 20 months, and acquire syntax completely at 48 to 60 months. All children pass these "milestones" and essentially at these same ages. They do so regardless of the language they acquire, or the circumstances under which they acquire it.

This neat-looking model of Lenneberg's does not seem to account for the findings of studies indicating that the under-privileged child is seriously handicapped at the time of admission to elementary school; his scores on standardized tests of intelligence are depressed and his speech and language skills are viewed by many teachers and others as being deviant and representing a protoype of "lower-class" communication patterns (Deutsch, 1963; John, 1963; Hess, Shipman, and Jackson, 1964) . Since the speech and language patterns of the school system are geared to middle-class standards of usage (Deutsch, 1963) , children having limited familiarity with these patterns are handicapped from the very start in their attempts to effect adequate communication. Thus, a vicious series of circuitous interrelationships is set into motion and a network of critical learning deficits begins to emerge. The handicap exists not only in their spoken language but in their reading and writing as well. Specifically, in addition to differences in syntactic structures, the culturally deprived child develops differences in dialect, generally with particular emphasis on vocabulary, grammar, and general word pronunciation, which complicate and interfere with communication and learning.

Implicit in the evolution of transformational grammar has been the distinction between *what* and *how* in studying language acquisition. This standard empirical assumption has also been made in differentiating the study of language from language performance. The study of language is an attempt to characterize an *ideal* normative model of a particular language. Language performance, on the other hand, is a matter of how a normative model is executed in actualized behavior. The distinction between the idealized competence of a speaker-listener (the what) and his actual performance (the how) has produced highly provocative and informative data for what a child learns in acquiring the syntax of language (McNeill, 1966; Slobin, 1966; Bellugi, 1965; Brown, 1965; Braine, in press). Work on the acquisition of syntax clearly demonstrates that attempts to describe what the child is learning do offer hints regarding how the child learns an open, infinite system such as language.

The development of phonological, morphological, and syntactical skills in the young child represents a major concern for a number of reasons. First, there are vital theoretical issues having to do with the manner by which language is acquired and the relationship between verbal and other cognitive skills. When we know more about how children of varying backgrounds acquire language and how their language skills interact with their abilities to perform other functions, we shall know a great deal about how to structure the educational environment to their best advantage. Next, we are interested in the verbal skills of these children because a good picture of these skills will indicate the nature of any deficit that might characterize them. We shall then be able to relate deficits to other conditions of their lives in order to search out the bases of the deficits. We need to know if the deficit is a matter of the verbal environment in which the children exist, a matter of reduced skills in conceptualization reflected in speech, or a matter of interpersonal problems that interfere with the social-communication components of verbal behavior (that is, the children have something to say but they have difficulty in saying it to the examiner or in making themselves understood).

Another reason why we must be interested in the verbal behavior of the preschool population is that we wish to identify more explicitly the impact of formal preschool- or headstart-type experiences in dialect. One might expect a significant improvement in dialect following a reasonable length of time spent in a verbally oriented environment where standard English is spoken. This might be so because of the increased range of exposure and learning opportunities with which the child comes in contact in formal school or pre-school settings as compared to the range found in many impoverished lower socioeconomic home environments. The extent that these referents are distinguishable verbally as well as behaviorally for the child is also the extent to which the child might have increased his standard English vocabulary in a number of syntactical categories. Although this may have some advantages to the child when he reaches the first grade, it is again not at all clear that he could not acquire this greater facility with standard English and an increased vocabulary very rapidly with appropriate techniques in the first grade. It might be, of course, that the greatest benefit of broadened preschool experiences lies not in the additional vocabulary developed, but in the cognitive advantages that might result from a larger vocabulary. For example, to be able to use a wide variety of color names means not only that the child can make finer discriminations among objects than he could with a more restricted vocabulary, but also that the notion of a *dimension* construed of a range of subcategories (that is, a concept) becomes available to the child. It is this relation between the acquisition of conceptual skills and the acquisition of verbal skills that represents one of our central problems.

REVIEW OF LITERATURE

In order to understand the acquisition of language, it is essential to understand something of what is acquired and what is already known about the role of environment. This necessarily includes study of the three main components of the grammar: (1) syntax, (2) semantics, and (3) phonology. In studying syntax, we study the structural relation of the linguistically permissible word sequence; in semantics, we study the content sequence; and in phonology, we study and describe the phoneme sequence.

The normal development of language strongly suggests the operation of a maturation process, as Lenneberg (1967) has argued. The complete absence of language in children deprived of all linguistic experience equally suggests a process of learning. The amount of linguistic experience, dependent on the nature of family and social motivations, is therefore a significant variable. Moreover, although both learning and maturation are necessary conditions for the development of language, neither is sufficient alone. To explain the obviously complex interrelationships, McNeill argues (1968) that we must consider the innate and acquired aspects of linguistic competence, as well as the situations in which they combine.

Chomsky's (1966) model of language acquisition tackles the problem quite elegantly. He sees "no conceivable question about the necessity for distinguishing competence from performance." This separation is essential for constructing generative grammar, and it is widely understood that no linguistic data are of much relevance unless they are collected from the generative grammar viewpoint.

With Chomsky's model in mind, recent studies of the development of syntax can be organized in terms of three contrasting strategies: (1) Observers have examined either the production or comprehension of speech. (2) They have attempted either to trace general linguistic advancement or the emergence of particular grammatical systems. (3) They have either conducted experimental studies or made observations of spontaneous linguistic behavior.

Of the eight possible categories of methods formed in this way, only four have been used at all, and most studies have used just two. There have been no studies, for example, of general comprehension. Most have worked with spontaneous linguistic production, following either the development of general linguistic competence or of particular linguistic systems. There have been no studies seriously attempting to relate linguistic development to intellectual development—which is a substantive issue.

The richest details and the deepest insights have so far come from longitudinal studies. Such studies have followed general linguistic development as well as the emergence of particular grammatical systems.

Almost without exception, observational studies have been engaged in the production and not the comprehension of speech. All are descendants of the early diary studies long conducted by newly parental linguists (Stern and Stern, 1907; Leopold, 1939, 1947, 1949a, 1949b) and differ from the earlier work mainly in the use of other people's children and in the collection of tape-recorded protocols. Braine (1963), Weir (1962), Brown and Bellugi (1964), Miller and Ervin (1964), McNeill (1966), and Gruber (1967) have all contributed in varying amounts to this literature. The ultimate step in such extralinguistic record keeping is placing everything on film or video tape, a step taken by Bullow, Jones, and Bever (1964).

One strategy is to write a grammar that describes a child's complete corpus. The hope in this case is to capture his total linguistic system at the time the corpus was collected, without distortion from adult grammar.

There is a serious question whether or not theory of competence can ever be developed from manipulations of a corpus (performance). Contemporary linguists deny that it can be done (Chomsky, 1964). A distributional analysis is a summary of performance, which at best provides a description of a child's grammatical classes, plus some hints as to his grammatical rules. A theory of competence remains unaccounted for.

It is possible to carry the second strategy to the level of true experimentation. Instead of observing the spontaneous occurrences of particular grammatical features, one tries to evoke them. For example, to test a child's comprehension of negation used in "what" questions, a child can be shown an array of objects—a boy, a doll, an orange, an apple, a ball, a toy, a tomato, and an ash tray—and be asked, "What can the little boy eat?" or "What can't the little boy eat?"

Perhaps the best known test of children's productive abilities is the test devised by Berko (1958). A comparable test has been independently developed by Bogoyavlenskiy (1957) for use with Russian children. Berko investigated the development of the morphological inflections of English: plural marking of nouns, past tense marking of verbs, comparative marking of adjectives, and some others.

The relation between the theory of grammar and children's innate linguistic capacities is simple and straightforward (McNeill, 1966). Languages have all necessarily evolved so as to correspond to children's capacities. No language can evolve to be unlearnable. Because children automatically impose those features of language that reflect their capacities, such features appear universally.

What are the universals mentioned in the theory of grammar that we now presume to be a reflection of children's innate capacities? Although some are syntactic, most universals describe characteristics of the deep structure of sentences (Chomsky, 1965) . Every language utilizes the same basic syntactic categories, arranged in the same way—such categories as sentences, noun phrases, verb phrases, etc. Every language utilizes the same basic grammatical relations among these categories—such relations as subject and predicate of a sentence, verb and object of a verbal phrase, etc. And every language distinguishes deep and surface structure and so is transformational.

Some universals are phonological. Every language, for example, employs consonant and vowel types, syllabic structure, and not more than fifteen distinctive features (Jakobson and Halle, 1956; Halle, 1964) . Other universals may be semantic—universals that are essentially constraints on possible concepts, on what is thinkable (Katz, 1966) .

If a language is acquired through discovering the transformations that relate surface structures to the universal aspects of the deep structure of sentences, then the latter must be present in children's earliest speech. Only differences in rate of maturation could affect this expectation.

There is a fundamental aspect of the discovery of transformations. Bringing deep and surface structures together for a child makes the discovery of a transformation possible. But the transformation must be then formulated. Doing so is the heart of learning language.

Universal transformational relations can be regarded as a set of general hypotheses available to children to explain the interrelations of the deep and surface structures that are displayed to them. The displays may be arranged through parent-child exchanges. Thus, it is evident that parents play an important role in acquisition of language.

The starting point of grammar is more or less the same for all children. Being universal, child grammar is not the grammar of any language, but is instead something that can become the grammar of any language through a process of formulating and modifying linguistic hypotheses.

In so evolving, language for a child moves from a maximally diffuse to a maximally articulated state. It starts with an ultimate and extremely general relation between sound and meaning; it progresses from there to a less intimate and general relation mediated by a deep structure semantics; semantic development is the most pervasive and the least understood aspect of language acquisition. However, theories of semantics are currently under active development, and matters in this quarter may soon improve (Katz and Foder, 1963; Katz and Postal, 1964; Katz, 1966, 1967; Weinreich, 1963, 1966).

Studies of statistical or normative nature are those which have to do with children's word associations (for example, di Vesta, 1964a, 1964b; Riegel, 1965; Piaget and Feldman, 1967; Riegel and Zivian, 1967) and children's ratings on the semantic differential (for example, di Vesta, 1966; di Vesta and Dick, 1966).

The more important studies of semantic aspects will be dealing with the semantic features of language. However, a major obstacle faced in the study of semantic development is a sweeping ignorance on the part of psycholinguists. Very few features have been isolated, and the procedure for discovering them is difficult and slow. Recently, Miller has devised a method, based on word-sorting and cluster-analysis, that yields categories of words not unlike the categories defined by the semantic features of linguistics. Slobin (1963, 1966) performed an experiment with children of five, seven, nine, and eleven years, in which truth of sentences was judged against pictured scenes.

In general, the success of children's messages to other children is low. Children use shorter descriptions than adults do, and the descriptions are sometimes highly idiosyncratic. Idiosyncratic messages are not meaningless, however, even though they are poor for communication; when children serve as their own decoders, the level of accuracy is relatively high (Glucksberg et al, 1966). It would appear, therefore, that children are better at decoding than encoding messages. However, children as decoders do not treat the communicative messages of adults differently from the noncommunicative messages of other children. All messages are accepted passively and with little comment. Children as encoders do not modify messages when explicitly requested to do so by adult decoders. In this respect, children are sharply different from adults (Glucksberg and Krauss, in press).

Two rather prominent theories exist for learning phonology by children. One theory is concerned with *what,* the other with *how.* Jakobson (1941) postulated that instead of attempting to find the order in which children acquire phonemes, it is necessary to discover the order in which they learn phoneme "contrasts." The notion of "contrast" learning suggests that segmental phonology (vowels and consonants) is acquired by learning successive maximal contrasts between the distinctive features that identify a particular phoneme or a set of phonemes. Little is known about the distinctive features of the suprasegmental system of phonology (Bolinger, 1964; Lieberman, 1966); however, the features of the segmental system have received considerable attention (Jakobson, Fant, Halle, 1952; Halle, 1964; Miller and Nicely, 1955).

The theory concerned with *how* is that of Mowrer (1960). He postulates that the learning of the sound system of language is no different than other forms of classical conditioning and, therefore, can be explained by the same model.

Both the theory of Jakobson and the classical conditioning paradigm have stimulated research on the acquisition of a sound system. The Jakobson approach is best exemplified by a Russian study by Shvachkin (1948). In a longitudinal study of children between one and two years of age, he found an ontogenetic sequence of phonemic differentiation that followed closely the predictions of Jakobson. Diary studies have also supported the phonemic "contrast" thesis. More recently, attempts have been made to characterize the vocal output of very young children by a modified distinctive feature classification (Sharf et al, 1967; Markel, 1967; Ringwall et al, 1965; Lane, 1965; Sheppard and Lane, 1966; Tikofsky, 1967). These systems for analyzing vocal output have followed closely recent advancements in distinctive feature theory (Jakobson and Halle, 1956; Halle, 1964).

The classical conditioning approach has resulted in attempts to reinforce vocal behavior by using different types of reinforcing conditions (Rheingold, et al, 1959; Weisberg, 1963). The results generally agree that quantitative changes can be demonstrated as a result of reinforcement.

A hierarchical concept of language suggests that the choice and arrangement of phonological sequences do not take place without consideration of the morphemic, syntactic, and semantic structure. Further, Chomsky (1966) suggests that in determining the derivational history of an utterance it is necessary to postulate an underlying as well as a surface representation of that utterance. The underlying or deep structure is represented by a semantic component and the surface structure is represented by a phonetic component.

Recent interest in infant behavior has provided some methodological cues in developing nonverbal indices for measuring responses to a variety of stimuli. For example, Frantz (1961) and Kagan and Lewis (1946) have described the value of fixation time and cardiac changes as measures of the "intensity" of attention to stimuli. Perceptual development seems to be accompanied by increased attention to partial violations or distortions of familiar patterns. This general finding leads to several experimental considerations using different languages as stimulus material. However, it has also been demonstrated by Frantz (1963) that stimulus preference may also result in longer fixation times. The work of Bower (1965) also suggests that "orienting reflex" responses can be used as a measure of attention to familiar and nonfamiliar stimuli.

Very little work in infancy has been done with auditory stimuli. The work of Eisenberg et al (1964) is a noted exception. Moreover, except for Kagan and Lewis' (1964) manipulation of meaning and inflection in verbal stimuli presented to young children (six months to thirteen months), linguistic cues have received little attention.

Following the assumption made earlier, it seems that the development of what children learn in distinguishing and sequencing phonemes could be studied until near seven years of age (Templin, 1957). Speech perception models offer some direction for predicting resultant changes or modifications of speech stimuli (Halle and Stevens, 1964; Wathen-Dunn, 1967). These models are basically input-output models which have provided valuable data in neurophysiology.

In the model proposed by Halle and Stevens (1964), speech production is described as a sequence of discrete units that are translated into vocal tract configurations which in turn produce the acoustic signal (Fant, 1960). In learning to speak a language, a speaker stores in his permanent memory a table of phonemes and their vocal tract configurations. Some phonemes may require more configurations than others and one particular configuration might be assigned to more than one phoneme. The latter possibility would account for allophonic variation. For example, the /k/ in *keep* is different from the /k/ in *kool,* but both are variants of the same phoneme /k/. A timing device is also postulated to account for different temporal changes within and between configurations. For example, the vowel in *meat* is shorter than the vowel in *mead.*

As a listener, the speaker must also store a list of acoustical properties that specify a phoneme. This process is seen as the reverse of speech production governed by the same set of generative rules. This requirement reduces the load on memory since the same set of rules or descriptions governs both speech production and speech recognition. Adding the concept of distinctive features to the generative rules further reduces the memory load by storing twelve to fifteen binary oppositions rather than each individual phoneme of a language.

The model would predict that in learning segmental phonemes and their configurations, the child will change the input signal by the smallest factor possible, given his internalized set of phonemic rules and their combinations. Morehead (1967) has found that this model predicts quite well the linguistic behavior of children as young as four years of age for processing sequencing rules such as those proposed by Whorf (1956) ; that is, a CCVC sequence that violates the internalized representation of the child will be changed by a small number of phonemes, each of which varies from the original phonemes in the sequence by only one to two distinctive features. Messer (1967) reports similar findings.

This evidence suggests that input-output models can predict the linguistic behavior of children. Moreover, it appears to be an excellent method for testing certain theoretical concepts regarding the learning of segmental phonology. For example, when young children are presented an impossible and unreal sequence such as /sr m/, the most frequent response is /sr m/. Association theories or concepts or meaningfulness and familiarity would not predict /sr m/, but rather a change to /dr m/ or /kr m/. It is unlikely that most children have ever heard /sr m/; thus, following these theories, the response could not be predicted as a possible response. Further, it would be impossible to predict this response without considering linguistic description of the structure of English. When this description is taken into account along with distinctive feature theory, then /sr m/ is a totally predictable response. The experimental power of a model that describes the structure of the input is that it allows more exact quantification of the expected changes in the output. This condition is a basic prerequisite to studying questions of *what* is learned, while manipulation of the output alone attempts to answer the *how* of learning. Failure to take into account the what before the how has resulted in postulating theories of language behavior that are incompatible with what is known about the infinite system of language.

5. SOCIAL DIALECT AND LANGUAGE*

Thomas H. Shriner

As is often mentioned, one major attribute of man is his ability to communicate with his fellow man. Far more than a means of communication, language in particular has become one of the principal means of thought, memory, introspection, and problem-solving, and it is related to all other mental activities. Educated man, in particular, should be articulate or at least moderately articulate in the speech patterns of his community. If he fails to meet certain proficiencies or has certain deviations from socially accepted speech patterns, his speech is usually referred to as substandard and he is placed into nonacceptable categories, or thought to be unequal.

Quite obviously, variations in articulation (pronunciation) exist both within and between different speech communities. Perhaps not relevant to this paper are the variations that exist between different speech communities, which are referred to as dialect-pronunciations. Dialect-

* The preparation of this paper was supported by Public Health Service Research Grant NB–07346 from the National Institute of Mental Health.

pronunciations are regional variations that may or may not be "socially different" when contrasts are made among various speech communities. Regional variations that do not fall into the "socially different" category should, in my opinion, not only be considered quite normal for that particular community, but also should be considered normal across speech community boundaries. One, for example, need only recall the dialect-pronunciations of our late President or listen to our current President. In these two examples, one may contend that particular dialect patterns may have certain merits and advantages.

Probably one purpose of this conference is to determine the extent to which these deviations become substandard or socially different when compared to Standard American English. Williams (1967) in an extensive review of the literature on language and poverty generalized that dialect or language differences have known associations with social stratifications, and also stated that it has been demonstrated that a person's dialect can be a reliable basis for classifying his social status. Thus, substandard speech appears to be characteristic of the poor or, more formally, the culturally disadvantaged.[1]

Much has been written and many studies have been completed comparing the language of the culturally disadvantaged child with that of his more privileged peers on such speech measures as sentence length and complexity, vocabu-

[1] Hurst and Jones (1966) were concerned with a more precise definition of substandard speech, poor speech, dialect, etc. They state that speech referred to under these headings involves such oral aberrations as phonemic and subphonemic replacements, segmental phonemes, phonetic distortion, defective syntax, misarticulations, mispronunciations, faulty phonology, and unintelligibility which can be found singly or in combinations. To refer to the subvariables mentioned above they prefer the term dialectolalia.

lary, or tasks of verbal comprehension. According to Gussow (1965) such studies have consistently indicated the existence of a quantitative deficit among the disadvantaged, though the factors of sex, age, IQ, and other variables such as the ethnic identity of the experimenter appear to affect the results significantly and often unpredictably. Overall, though, such studies would seem to indicate that low social status actually does have a quantitatively depressing effect on certain forms of language production. Gussow (1965) further states that these children know conventional names for fewer things, whether objects or actions; they have a more restricted grammatical range, and produce simpler sentences. But language goes beyond verbal communication, as mentioned in the opening paragraph, and consists of a good deal more than countable, audible items.

That language in some form does exist among the culturally disadvantaged cannot be denied; culturally disadvantaged children learn the language of their particular region and appear to learn to function in that particular speech community quite well. It is only when they cross speech-community boundaries and contrasts are made with the culturally advantaged that they become socially different. Gussow stated quite appropriately: "What is undoubtedly and unfortunately true is that a good deal more effort has been expended on modifying the pronunciation and syntax of lower-class speech than has been expended on improving language functioning for these children." In my opinion, this suggests that we adopt a viewpoint which not only is concerned with dialectolalia (as defined by Hurst and Jones) *per se,* but emphasizes the improvement of language functioning for these children. Language problems should be considered more fundamental than speech problems and only after the child has made significant gains in language development should he be referred for speech therapy. According to Gussow, there are several respects in which speech therapy appears questionable. If we are really concerned with social acceptance, we have very little information on the kinds of "corrections" that should be emphasized. We do not know which phonological deviations, which syntactical "errors," or which lexical substitutions have the most negative effect on the listener. We do not know which interfere the most with social mobility and which kinds of standard speech, if any, we should teach. The emphasis on correct speech appears to be questionable if there is no improvement in language behavior. If we are to be concerned with maximum development, we must recognize that a child's language is not merely related to the way he speaks but to the way he thinks. Highly relevant is the Whorfian hypothesis that all higher levels of thinking are dependent on language and that the structure of the language one habitually uses influences the manner in which one understands his environment—the picture of the universe shifts from tongue to tongue. To quote quite liberally from Gussow, low status dialect may hamper the child's social mobility, but a restricted language development may limit his intellectual potential. It has often been assumed that the culturally disadvantaged child's ability to use language as a cognitive tool is impaired in proportion to his inability to communicate in Standard English. Gussow in 1965 stated that the question is unanswered as to whether most substandard dialects do provide language structures and resources adequate to the needs of complex communicative or problem solving tasks. Williams in 1967 in a review of the literature stated that the following generalizations seemed evident about the culturally disadvantaged child:

A poverty environment has a socializing influence upon its population, an influence which manifests itself in distinctions of language and cognition, and these distinctions in turn serve in the definition and perception of the population as a poverty culture.

Constituent generalizations include:

A. The language of a "poverty" or "disadvantaged" class symptomizes a perceptual restriction to the nonabstract—to that which is directly, personally, and grossly experienced, and only limited recognition of higher levels of conceptualization.

B. The socializing influence of poverty upon language and cognition begins in early childhood.

C. Unless the socializing influence is somehow modified in early childhood, the language and cognitive capabilities of the child may be susceptible to a cumulative deficit.

D. Limited verbal capabilities are often seen as the most evident deficit in both preschool and school children from poverty or disadvantaged populations.

E. Special preschool or school programs tend to have some desirable consequences upon children from poverty populations.

F. Programs designed to evaluate and to remedy problems presumably due to poverty or class differences must guard against confusing that which is culturally different from that which is culturally deficient.

G. Language characteristics of a population may be a major barrier to their successful integration into a particular society or occupation.

H. Dialects or language differences have known associations with social stratification, and it has been demonstrated that a person's dialect can be a reliable basis for classifying his social status.

If we accept the premise that language consists of a good

deal more than quantifiable, audible items and further accept the Whorfian hypothesis of linguistic relativity, then perhaps we should view the substandard speech of the culturally disadvantaged as a psycholinguistic problem. Methods derived from recent developments in linguistics and/or neobehaviorism appear to me to be the most fruitful avenue for studying the language structure of these children and also the most fruitful for remedial teaching (if thought desirable).

Relevant to this paper is the linguistic competence-performance model and, more specifically, the application of this model to the study of the culturally disadvantaged child's language structure. (For a more thorough discussion of competence vs performance, see Chomsky; Cazden; McNeill; Wales and Marshall; Fodor and Garrett.) Briefly, in the case of language, competence is the speaker-listener's knowledge of his language. The speaker-listener has an internalized system of rules that are finite and enable him to comprehend and produce an infinite (theoretically) number of sentences. A grammar is a representation of competence constructed by linguists of such a system of rules. Performance is the expression of competence in speaking or listening; that is, how we actually put it to use, realize and express it. One is competent to deal with an infinite number of grammatical sentences, but one's performance may be distracted in various ways. In other words, a study of performance gives clues to competence. McNeill (1967) states, with respect to language acquisition, that our concern should be with competence, for only after we have understood this to some degree can we hope to understand performance.

If we are to be concerned with the language of the disadvantaged child, then we should determine whether differences exist in competence for the particular language he has learned, relative to the competence of a comparable speaker-listener's language that we think socially acceptable. (For an excellent discussion of individual differences in competence, see Cazden, 1967.) But, as Cazden has mentioned, the design of an experimental situation that successfully probes for children's knowledge creates certain problems; that is, it is extremely difficult to devise tests of linguistic competence.

In an attempt to assess, in part, the culturally disadvantaged child's morphological competence, a study was designed by Shriner and Miner. It was assumed that once a child has learned a morphological rule, he can apply this rule to unfamiliar situations. Our specific purpose was to compare two groups of preschool children—culturally disadvantaged with culturally advantaged—in their ability to apply morphological rules to unfamiliar situations. Our general method consisted of constructing a thirty-item morphology test, adapted from the techniques employed by Brown (1957), Berko (1958), and Cooper (1967). The test, both expressive and receptive parts, was administered to twenty-five culturally disadvantaged and twenty-five culturally advantaged children. The receptive test was administered after the expressive test had been completed so that the subjects would not receive initially a correct model which might influence their production on the expressive test.

The subjects in the experimental group were twenty-five white, midwestern, culturally disadvantaged children. There were fifteen males and ten females. They were from very low income families and were participating in a nursery school program while their parents were participating in a federally sponsored vocational training program. Participation by the children in the nursery school program and the parents in the vocational training program was compulsory if the parents wished to continue receiving financial aid from the government. Each subject was first administered the Peabody Picture Vocabulary Test, Form A, to determine his mental age. A picture articulation test, constructed by the authors, was then given to test for those phonological items included on the morphology test. The purpose of this articulation test was to eliminate those subjects who may have had omissions of the items under study. Furthermore, if a child had a sound phoneme substitution, /θ-s/ for example, the substitution was considered correct at the morphologic level, even though it was incorrect at the phonemic level.

The chronological age range of the children was from two years, seven months to six years, one month, with a mean age of four years, four months. The mental age range was from two years, four months to six years, six months, with a mean age of three years, ten months.

The control group was twenty-five advantaged children participating in a private nursery school in the same community. Each child came from a middle-class environment as judged by the nursery school teacher's knowledge of occupations and types of home in which the children lived. The advantaged children also were administered the Peabody Picture Vocabulary Test and the articulation test. They were matched to the disadvantaged children on the basis of sex and mental age (± three months) . A total of sixty-three advantaged children were tested before appropriate matchings could be made. Controlling mental age was considered especially important. It was assumed that mental age as opposed to chronological age would be more indicative of the child's present level of linguistic competence and also of his ability to apply that knowledge. Partial support for this assumption is given by Zeaman and House (1966). In their review of the relation of IQ and learning, they state that chronological age appears to be an irrelevant variable for learning and cite a number of studies to this effect.

The chronological age range of the children was from three years, five months to five years, eight months, with a mean age of four years, eight months. The mental age range was from two years, four months to six years, six months, with a mean age of four years, two months. The mean IQ for the advantaged children was 89.3 and the mean IQ for the disadvantaged children was 89.7.

Expressive knowledge of morphological rules was tested by requiring each child to auditorially close a statement with certain contextual clues. The examiner, for example, would state, "Here is a geep." (Nonsense figure is displayed on a card.) "Here is another geep." (A second card is displayed adjacent to the first card depicting the same visual stimulus.) "Now there are two————." If the subject uttered "geeps," evidence existed that he had productive ability to apply a generative rule for, in this instance, pluralizations.

The expressive test consisted of twenty items, including ten noun pluralizations, six verb forms, and four possessives. The stimuli were nonsense syllables which attempted to minimize possible phonological difficulties by utilizing only syllables which ended in a final /p/, /b/, /t/, /d/, /m/, or /i/. In the case of the nouns, the subjects were required to generate two past tense items, /nob + d/; and two third-person-singular items /mip + s/ were tested. Two singular and two plural forms of the possessive were employed.

Only the pluralization of nouns was tested receptively in this study. For this test, each child was given both an auditory stimulus (singular form of the noun) and a visual one (plate with nonsense pictures) and required to execute a nonverbal response (pointing). Each plate contained a picture of the stimulus word, the correct pluralized noun, and three foils, one of which was just the singular form of the stimulus word. It was assumed that auditory-reception was of more significance than visual-reception. This assumption seems reasonable because, if the child did not have receptive knowledge of the morphological rule, he would have visually matched the singular stimulus word with the singular foil. The examiner, for example, would state, "See this. This is a gat. Now look at these pictures. Since this is a gat, point to gats." The position of the correct answer was randomly distributed among the four possible positions.

A comparison of the total morphology test scores between the culturally disadvantaged children and the culturally advantaged children revealed no statistically significant difference. The resulting t-ratio (1.20, df = 24) is nonsignificant at the .05 level of confidence. Both groups increased in their ability to apply the morphological rules to unfamiliar situations as a function of increased mental age. In no instance did any child get all the items correct. The range was from two to twenty-seven items correct.

Since all variables thought relevant were controlled except chronological age, the difference between the mean chronological age of the experimental group and the mean chronological age of the control group was evaluated. The resulting t-ratio (0.16, df = 40) is nonsignificant, less than 1.00.

In an effort to locate possible significant differences obscured by pooling mean scores for all children in the experimental and control groups, additional computations were made with other variables. Within-group and between-group comparisons were made which looked for differences in sex, subtest items, and receptive vs expressive abilities. As indicated in table 1, none of the resulting t-ratios approached statistical significance at the .05 level. There was no statistically significant difference on the performance of the morphology test by males vs females both within and between groups.

There was no statistically significant difference in the performance of the experimental vs the control group on the various subtest items. No differences in the ability to apply receptive nouns, expressive nouns, verb forms, or possessives emerged between the disadvantaged and advantaged children.

Within-group comparisons were made relative to receptive vs expressive pluralization abilities. No statistically significant differences resulted in the receptive vs expressive production scores for either group.

The authors think it highly significant that no significant results emerged from this investigation. Several hypotheses are discussed that may account for the lack of significant results between culturally disadvantaged and culturally advantaged children on a test of morphological skills. One hypothesis would be that actual morphological differences exist between the experimental and control groups. It is merely that the morphology test constructed for use in this study was not sensitive enough to measure these differences. This notion, however, appears untenable, because the mean scores increase with an increase in mental age, suggesting basic test validity.

A second interpretation is that it is extremely difficult to test or describe a child's linguistic competence, as mentioned previously, since linguistic competence cannot be observed directly. If linguistic competence were not properly assessed, then no significant differences would be expected. Nonsense words, presumably, are unique stimuli for testing competence because they require each subject to generate an unfamiliar response on the basis of an internalized system of rules, thus eliminating the experimental factor of memory for items under test. One may argue that observationally the child's performance may vary with various factors, such as time of day, emotional state of the child or the examiner, physical condition of the child or examiner, or, more importantly in this situation, familiarity or meaningfulness of the nonsense words used to elicit the various responses. It must be remembered that even nonsense syllables or words have varying degrees of meaningfulness (Mednick, 1964, p. 6; Nobel, 1961, p. 149; Glaze, 1928). Furthermore, Ervin (1964, p. 174) has stated that a child will employ the plural suffix with some consistency with *familiar* words before he generalizes to new words. To quote Ervin, "Thus, between the time when the child contrasted *block* and *blocks* and the time when he said that two things called *bik* were *biks*, there was a small but reliable gap of about two weeks. For *car* and *boy* and the analogous *kie*, the gap was about six weeks. For other words the gap was greater." It may appear that the second interpretation is tenable; namely, that competence was not assessed. It is assumed by the authors that competence was assessed to a large degree by using nonsense words because morphological mean scores improved with increased mental age.

One may also ask whether the two groups were really matched on mental age. It may be contended that the disadvantaged child was penalized because the Peabody Picture Vocabulary Test is a measure of receptive vocabulary. Because the disadvantaged child probably does lack vocabulary development, a different nonverbal, nonvocabulary test may have shown higher mental age scores; therefore, each child's true ability was not tapped. If the assumption is made that the disadvantaged child's mental age was not assessed, then, in all probability, their mental ages are higher than the children who were in the control group. If this were so, however, it would have been reflected in the results, the disadvantaged child's score being systematically higher than the advantaged child's score. Statistical analysis did not reveal this.

Because all variables thought relevant were controlled, and no significant differences were found between the experimental and control groups, it is concluded that disadvantaged and advantaged children do not differ in terms of the morphological rules measured by this study. This is not to say that culturally disadvantaged children do not have specific morphological language problems. This study did not assess whether the culturally disadvantaged or the culturally advantaged have morphological learning disabilities. It is concluded, however, that this study did assess both groups' ability to apply morphological competence to unfamiliar situations. Perhaps studies of larger populations of culturally disadvantaged and culturally advantaged children may reflect specific morphological language differences, or perhaps the labels "culturally disadvantaged" and "culturally advantaged" are misnomers when relevant variables are controlled.

In my opinion, this study needs to be repeated on larger and different populations that are considered socially different. The competence-performance model should be applied to other aspects of the structure of language; syntax and cognitive process, in particular, need to be investigated before instructional methods (if thought desirable) become thoroughly effective. It is recognized, however, that instructional methods are quite often initiated before research has established specific deficits or avenues of approach. The educator or speech-language clinician utilizing clinical intuition feels that something must be done, and proceeds without adequate models or guidelines. This has been especially true with respect to the culturally disadvantaged population.

A conceptual framework for assessment, grouping, and instruction for any given child with a learning disability has been proposed recently by the director of our Children's Research Center, Dr. Herbert C. Quay. (I will be quoting quite liberally from his paper.) This conceptual framework can be used by the educator in classroom teaching or used by the speech-language clinician once specific language deficiencies are noted; that is, it is a framework aimed at improving those aspects of the learning process in which the child may suffer a disability.

According to Quay, the elements of such a system should be variables related to the learning process that can be manipulated by the educator or speech-language clinician. While constructs or models are valuable in theoretical explanations of learning and offer schemes for integrating data, they are inferred from stimulus-response relationships and are not directly manipulable. Auditory association, for example, may help explain some facet of poor performance in the learning process, but it is only stimulus, response, and reinforcement variables that can be manipulated to improve auditory association.

The framework offered by Quay consists of a set of functions and the relation of these functions to certain modalities of the learning parameters of input, response, and reinforcement. If and when specific language learning disabilities of the culturally disadvantaged child are known, then the interaction of these three components provides a basis for a technology of instruction. His framework is presented schematically in table 2. As can be noted, there are 41 cells, each of which represents the point of interaction of a function and modality with a parameter of learning. Each cell represents a behavior that can be measured to yield a quantitative estimate for a given child. Once measured, some intervention (remedial technology) may be initiated for its remediation. Table 2 will not be discussed in any detail and it is presented only as additional information. By way of example, though, orientation refers to the basic necessity for the child to be oriented toward the stimulus for a response to it to occur. For example, the hyperactive child, who does not look at his worksheet clearly cannot perceive its contents, no matter how good his skills in the perceptual area. Neither can the child respond without orientation; he cannot write the spelling word on the page while looking out the window, nor respond orally to a question while talking to his neighbor. Finally, a reinforcer cannot operate without orientation toward it occurring. This scheme has many advantages which may be used to study the culturally disadvantaged population. Very little is known with respect to each of the cells about the special needs of this population. As stated earlier, very little is known about the culturally disadvantaged child's level of linguistic competence as compared with that of his more privileged peer. The framework proposed by Quay not only provides a method of assessment but also provides a basis for grouping children according to their special needs in terms of variables thought relevant. If and when these special needs are discovered, perhaps through use of the linguistic competence-performance model, and the variables thought relevant explored with respect to various socially different populations, then the Quay Scheme should prove to be highly significant for instructional purposes.

SUMMARY

My presentation was concerned with the social dialect (s) of the population described as being socially different, or, more formally, the culturally disadvantaged. I have suggested that we adopt a viewpoint that is not only concerned with their dialect patterns *per se,* but a viewpoint much larger in scope. Language problems should be considered more fundamental than speech problems, and only after a child has made significant gains in language development should he be referred for speech therapy. It was pointed out that very little is known about the language development of the culturally disadvantaged child and that instructional

TABLE 1.

Relationship of Morphology Scores to Other Variables with Resulting T-Ratio and Degree of Freedom for Each Comparison.

	Variable	Comparison	t-ratio*	df
SEX	Control Group	Male vs Female	.09	23
	Experimental Group	Male vs Female	.49	23
	Females	Exp. vs Cont.	.23	9
	Males	Exp. vs Cont.	1.13	14
SUBTEST ITEMS	Receptive Nouns	Exp. vs Cont.	.54	9
	Expressive Nouns	Exp. vs Cont.	1.27	9
	Verb Forms, Possessives	Exp. vs Cont.	1.52	9
RECEPTIVE VS	Experimental Group	Rec. vs Expr.	1.28	18
EXPRESSIVE	Control Group	Rec. vs Expr.	.90	18

* None of the resulting t-ratios approached statistical significance at .05.

methods, with respect to this population, have been initiated without the establishment of specific deficits or avenues of approach. I suggested that if we are to be concerned with the language of the disadvantaged child, then we should determine whether or not differences exist in competence for the particular language he has learned, relative to the competence of a comparable speaker-listener's language that we think socially acceptable. A conceptual framework for assessment, grouping, and instruction, proposed by a colleague, that can be applied to any given child in terms of variables thought relevant also was touched upon.

MODALITIES	INPUT				RESPONSE				REINFORCEMENT					
	Activity	Orientation	Perception	Failure to Score	Dexterity	Orientation	Organization	Delay	Activity	Orientation	Effect	Delay	Amt.	Ratio
Visual														
Auditory														
Tactual														
Motor														
Verbal														
Primary-Sensory														
Social														
Information														

TABLE 2
(After Quay)

6. ARTICULATORY ACQUISITION:
SOME BEHAVIORAL CONSIDERATIONS*

Harris Winitz

My concerns in this paper are exclusively with concepts and procedures that may prove to be useful in modifying speech sound behavior, whether of functional or of dialectical origin. The term "speech sound behavior" is a general term that includes phonetic behavior, phonemic status, and distributional differences at the phonemic and morphemic levels. No doubt much more than this is involved in speech learning, especially when one considers the new developments in the grammar of phonology. They will not, however, be discussed here.

We shall present below a descriptive outline of three response phases that may have merit for studying phonological learning. Before we do this, we will mention four behavioral processes that are part of each of the response phases. They are as follows:

(1) *Transfer of training.* In psychological theory, transfer is considered to be a general phenomenon that describes or considers a variety of stimulus and response events that

* Supported by Grant HD 01657 from the National Institute of Child Health and Human Development.

influence the learning of a second activity. Given an appropriate set of instances, positive transfer will result. An example of positive transfer at the phonetic level is the following sequence for learning [χ], a voiceless dorso-uvular fricative:

1. sn*
   ←
2. sn
   ←
   sn
   →
3. h
   ←
   sn
   →
4. [χɑ]

The principles of this program, which are no doubt obvious,
result in generalization or transfer of the necessary distinctive features for the utterance of the [χ] sound. With the
exception of this one example I have never devoted my
energies to this problem, although it seems worthy of study
from both theoretical and practical points of view.

(2) *Competition of Responses.* There is little in the psychological literature that will help us understand this problem, although for articulatory learning it is an important dimension. Response competition refers to the blocking or
obstruction of new sound learning by highly established responses. These old responses, which by definition are the incorrect responses, may be elicited by a variety of stimuli; for
example, distributional cues, morphemic constraints, and
phonetic and phonemic contexts. The incorrect response

* Where sn refers to an inspirated snore and sn to an expirated
snore. ←   →

may be one or more elements of the phoneme (that is, its distinctive features) or the phoneme itself.

(3) *Auditory Distinctiveness.* It is conceivable that in some instances speech sound responses may be learned without specialized instruction by using appropriate discrimination pretraining procedures. In our laboratory we have employed the successive discrimination paradigm: it is a two-alternative sound discrimination task. Sounds are presented in random order at five-second intervals and a child attempts to learn which sound corresponds to which of the two buttons or bars.

Difficult sound discriminations can be learned by utilizing the principle of distinctive stimulus pretraining. Learning of difficult discriminations can be effected by utilizing pretraining stimuli that are initially discriminable. In addition, the stimulus elements of the pretraining stimuli and of subsequent stimuli should be from the same stimulus dimension and as similar as possible. Stimulus elements that are both common and similar form the necessary ingredients for mediation and generalization, processes that are no doubt responsible for the effectiveness of pretraining with distinctive stimuli.

The general method is one in which an easy discrimination facilitates learning of a difficult discrimination. No further attempt will be made to give a theoretical accounting of distinctive stimulus pretraining since it is complex and not very well understood. Its efficacy, however, has been demonstrated with speech sounds in our laboratory (Winitz and Preisler, 1967), using second-graders as subjects. In this study the terminal contrastive pair was /br/–/vr/. The experimental group was pretrained on the /fr/–/br/ contrast, /fre/ vs /bre/, for 48 trials (six blocks of 8 trials); this group received 32 additional trials (four blocks of 8 trials) involving the /br/–/vr/ contrast; the stimuli were /vre/–/bre/; and the control group received 80 trials (ten blocks of 8 trials) on the /br/–/vr/ contrast (/bre/ vs /vre/). The experimental group benefited substantially from distinctive feature pretraining.

One factor that appears to be a critical component of this procedure is the order of the phonemes used in the training sequence. If the initial contrastive pair includes the correct sound, rather than the error sound, this procedure will not work (Winitz and Preisler, 1967). Presumably, the subject identifies the correct sound as the error sound, or an insignificant variation of the correct sound (allophone in free variation), and the sounds become equivalent during the discrimination sessions. Thus subjects in our experiment were unable to learn the /ʃ/–/ç/ contrast when /ө/ was paired with /ç/ rather than with /ʃ/ in the early stages of training. It should be mentioned that children most often utter /ʃ/ when they hear /ç/.

(4) *Retention of Articulatory Responses.* A greatly neglected consideration in articulatory pretraining is the dimension of forgetting. Elsewhere (Winitz, 1969) we have suggested that proactive interference seems to be the most appropriate paradigm for the study of articulatory retention, since older, more established responses are to be replaced by new responses. Presumably the subject brings to the clinic a set of highly learned responses which not only interferes with sound acquisition but affects recall as well. There is an analogue in verbal behavioral research.

Provided with an impressive accumulation of facts, Underwood in 1957 suggested that a good share of the forgetting that occurs in the laboratory may be attributed to events that antedate the laboratory exercise, especially when one observes the cumulative effects of multilist learning and relearning on retention. Since these antedating associations occur prior to the associations to be recalled and since they are not learned in a laboratory, Underwood and Postman refer to them as extraexperimental sources of interference—associations which the subjects bring to the laboratory and which are detrimental to the retention of new associations learned in the laboratory. The above considerations led Underwood and Postman to consider two sources of interference, letter sequences and unit sequences, that seemed amenable to experimental tests.

In the standard proactive interference (PI) paradigm, two lists are learned in the laboratory; the second list is tested for retention after an interval of time has passed. It can be pictured as follows:

PI Group: learn A–B;   learn A–C................recall A–C
                                          i   k   i   k
Control Group: learn A–C................recall A–C
                                          i   k   i   k

where A refers to stimuli, and B and C to responses. A–C recall is superior for the control group, since there is no competition from antedating responses.

When testing for extraexperimental sources of interference, the laboratory exercise involves the learning and retention of a single list. Lists are developed so as to maximize or minimize preexperimental associations. The associations are assumed to be the result of well-learned natural language habits (NLH) and are gleaned from normative data on associations or computed from their frequency of occurrence in the English language.

The sources of interference in the letter sequence hypothesis are intraunit and are presumed to operate in the following way. A trigram like "GHO" is relatively infrequent in English. During learning the covert elicitation of frequent trigrams like "GRO" and "GLO" needs to be extinguished. Recall would be difficult, because with the passage of time "GRO" and "GLO" would recover and compete with the recall of "GHO." "GRO" and "GLO" would not encounter this kind of competition and therefore should be recalled with little difficulty.

When this theory was originally proposed, no mention was made of the fact that high frequency trigrams may compete among each other to cause a reduction in recall. This consideration has not been tested with single lists, but experiments employing the traditional PI paradigm have not lent weight to this possibility (Postman, 1962; Underwood and Ekstrand, 1967). We are now investigating this situation with single lists in our laboratory.

The unit sequence hypothesis makes opposite predictions for items such as words. High interitem associations like *square-round, square-circle, square-block, square-box* produce competitive associations maximizing interference and retarding recall. Low frequency words like *lax* or *ado* represent items with a history of few associations and, therefore, interference should be minimal. Thus high associations are detrimental for the recall of words but beneficial for the recall of letter sequences. The interference gradients are summarized by Underwood and Postman (1960, pp. 75–76) as follows:

> The letter-sequence interference gradient will be at a maximum when the pre-experimental associative strength between letters is low. The amount of such interference will decrease as the pre-experimental associative connection between letters increases. When the associative connection between letters becomes of strength found among letters in low-frequency words, another gradient, the unit-sequence gradient, begins to emerge. The amount of interference ex-

pected from this gradient continues to increase up to the point where very high-frequency words are present.

Over a score of studies aimed at testing the above gradients of interference have given essentially no support to the theory of extraexperimental interference (see Underwood and Ekstrand, 1967). The experimental manipulations have involved a number of verbal behavioral techniques using essentially the list types mentioned above.

SEGMENTATION OF THE ARTICULATORY LEARNING PROCESS

With the above considerations in mind, we have most recently (Winitz and Bellerose, 1968), for experimental purposes, segmented articulatory learning into two major phases of learning: acquisition—learning of a "new" response pattern; and association—linking the newly acquired response to a stimulus.

Using trigrams we can illustrate these two phases most clearly. Thus, for example, learning the following stimulus-response pairs requires presumably first acquisition (or integration) and second association:

Stimulus		*Response*
1	–	XCN
2	–	VGX

"XCN" and "VGX" are trigrams which do not occur in English. Whereas for the following pairs only association learning is involved:

Stimulus		*Response*
1	–	TOT
2	–	BAB

The grapheme sequences "TOT" and "BAB" appear in words like "total" and "baby."

An outline of the response acquisition and response association phases is given below.

Response Acquisition

(A) Acquiring sounds that *are not* part of the language.
1. Some or all features may be available for transfer.
2. Competition is minimal, unless distinctive features overlap considerably.
3. Discrimination pretraining may not be necessary, but possibly may speed up the learning process.
4. Proactive interference is not a factor.

(B) Acquiring sounds that are part of the language.
1. Some or all features may be available for transfer; sounds may be available when the response is inconsistently correct.
2. Competition is maximal, as there is a history of error substitution.
3. Discrimination pretraining may be sufficient if all features are available.
4. Proactive interference impairs recall.

Response Association

1. The sound is available from the response acquisition phase.
2. Competition is from linguistic context and is assumed to be maximal.

3. Discrimination pretraining is effective and may be a sufficient condition for sound learning.

4. Proactive interference impairs recall.

Our own research endeavors have concentrated on discrimination pretraining and retention.

In the brief discussion that follows, we do not refer directly to dialect differences, but perhaps we can make the proper application later in the symposium. No direct mention is made of classical phonemic analysis since we are often concerned with the learning of a single response. In many ways, however, our outline does take into account phonemic status and distributional differences. The subjects in the studies to be reported were kindergarten, first-, second-, and third-grade children.

RESPONSE ACQUISITION

Acquiring Sounds Not Part of the Language

(1) *Transfer of features.* In one study (Winitz, 1969) subjects were divided into three groups: (a) perfect articulation (50 correct responses on the Templin-Darley Test), (b) errors of the /r/ phoneme, and (c) defective articulation (20 out of 50 on the Templin-Darley Test) including errors of the /r/ and /s/ phonemes. The learning task involved the /vr/ and /ʃm/ clusters. We predicted that on the /vr/ cluster the defective group and the /r/ error group would not differ and that their scores would be lower than those in the perfect group; and that on the /ʃm/ cluster the /r/ error group and the perfect group would not differ, and their scores would be superior to the defective group.

We did not obtain learning for the /vrow/ syllable (20 trials); however for the /ʃmeɪ/ syllable the findings were in the direction stated above. Here, then, is preliminary evidence for response transfer.

(2) *Competition.* We have conducted no study that bears directly on this question, except to say we have taught the phones [ç], [x], and [œ] to children and noted that these sounds can be learned (Winitz and Lawrence, 1961). The order of difficulty from easy to hard was [œ], [ç], and [x]. However, for obvious reasons we cannot make any general statements about response difficulty.

(3) *Discrimination pretraining.* In one study (Winitz and Bellerose, 1967) four subjects (two experimental and two control subjects) learned the /r–w/ and /r̪–w/ contrasts after about three weeks of discrimination training, one-half hour per day. No difference in /r/ production was observed after this extensive period of time.

A phonemic analysis was not made since all subjects showed no evidence of correct /r/ production. However, had the subjects been inconsistent in their error response and had a phonemic analysis given evidence of an [r] contrast, we would expect that discrimination pretraining might be sufficient for [r] transfer. This situation exemplifies response association learning, which will be considered below.

(4) *Retention.* We have no data here, although Rice and Milisen (1954) report that retention was inversely related to the length of the retention interval (one and 72 hours) for teenage subjects. They used the sounds [β], [ʒz], and [x].

Acquiring Sounds That Are Part of the Language

(1) *Transfer and competition.* We have no data here but we suspect that transfer will be minimal when competition is strong. In short, the rule may be the following:

When the distinctive features of the stimulus compound

(the phone) are available to the subject but have a low intrafeature association value, acquisition should be most rapid.

We have by analogy the findings of Underwood and Schulz that trigram learning was inversely correlated (−.78) with an interference index. The index was computed from the single letter transitional probabilities of the second and third letters and the item probability of the first letter. In this instance all letters were, of course, available to the subject, since this was an exercise with the English alphabet.

For sounds, it is difficult to conceive of a situation where distinctive feature availability would not be correlated with some kind of derived distinctive feature associative index. Note in particular that letter associations are linear whereas for sounds many of the features occur, for the most part, simultaneously. Thus, for the /b/ sound, voicing, stopping, and labial movements are for our purposes not a linear association but a "cluster" association. This point of view would not necessarily be a valid one for an acoustical phonetician.

It is possible, however, that the features of voicing, stopping, and bilabial placement, for example, may never have been conjoined. That is, consider a child who has no voiced stops and no voiced bilabial sounds. However, he may have a voiceless, bilabial fricative, a voiceless dorso-velar stop, and many voiced sounds. In this instance, we would expect that the production of the /b/ sound would take place with minimal interference and maximal transfer.

(2) *Discrimination pretraining.* Our findings to date do not suggest that discrimination pretraining, when distinct features are available, will result in correct articulatory productions without specialized articulatory training. The evidence we have is extremely limited, and is that reported for the /r/ phoneme above.

(3) *Retention*. For the articulatory acquisition stage, retention may be impaired for newly integrated units. The evidence from the verbal behavioral literature suggests that original learning (or interpolated learning in the standard PI paradigm) would be the critical variable and that, when this was controlled in the studies of extraexperimental sources of interference, the retention of newly integrated units (low frequency trigrams) does not differ from highly integrated units (high frequency trigrams) (Underwood and Ekstrand, 1967).

RESPONSE ASSOCIATION

(1) *Transfer and competition*. Once a sound has been acquired, positive transfer seems to be related to response competition, the latter being a serious problem in the response association phase. Competition may be from distributional sources; for example, subjects who substitute the [w] for the [r] sound in the same environments, say the initial position, would experience response competition. Minimization of the error sound would then be a critical dimension of the response association phase.

In some instances it is possible to minimize competition from distributional sources, when the word-unit is a non-English word. The plan here is to integrate the newly acquired sound into word units, sustaining its production over a specified time interval, and then gradually transferring it to English words.

Within this general framework, it was hypothesized that the development of an articulatory response would be facilitated when the speech unit does not evoke a previously learned word. It was assumed that the familiar word (mediating response), evoked by a similar verbal stimulus, would elicit an articulatory response to be learned and, thus, interfere with its acquisition. Some support for this hypothesis can be found from the fact that Scott and Milisen (1954) and Carter and Buck (1958) found that the use of nonsense-syllable material facilitated the correction of articulatory errors.

The subjects, first- and second-grade children, assigned initially to one of three groups, were instructed to learn to produce the stimulus /srə'b/, which was to be played from a tape recorder (Winitz and Bellerose, 1965). Pretesting had indicated that the majority of children responded to the stimulus /srə'b/ with the verbal unit /ʃrə'b/. The instructions for the three groups were as follows:

Group I: The subjects were shown a picture of a *shrub* and were told to learn to pronounce the word *shrub* in a different way.

Group II: The subjects were instructed to learn to say the *word* they were about to hear.

Group III: The subjects were shown a picture of some cable wires and were told that this was the name of something that goes in a television set and that they were to learn to say its name.

The findings indicate that subjects in Group III benefited from the pretraining instructions. Apparently orientation away from the word *shrub* and to a new "word" reduced the probability that /sr/ and /ʃr/ would be equated, thereby minimizing the interference of /ʃr/. Interestingly enough, the word *shrub* did not have to be identified for the subjects, as no difference was found between Groups I and II.

(3) *Discrimination pretraining.* If orientation to an incorrect perceptual unit retards articulatory learning, then discrimination training should prevent such orientation. Therefore, we decided to test the effects of discrimination

training on sound association learning (Winitz and Preisler, 1965).

The subjects were first-grade children, thirty in number, who on two successive days (21 trials per day) did not produce /sr/ when hearing /srə'b/. Instead, they uttered /skrəb/. (A few children said /ʃrə'b/ but the majority in this sample said /skr'əb/, and so to keep procedures uniform only children with the latter "error" were included.) The instructions they received pertained to the learning situation; that is, they were told to try their best to say the "sound" they heard on the tape recorder and that correct responses would be reinforced.

At the end of the second day, the subjects were divided into two groups: Group A received discrimination training on the /skr'əb/—/srə'b/ contrast while Group B received training on the neutral contrast /sliyp/–/ʃliyp/. The discrimination procedures were identical to those explained above (under *Auditory Distinctions*).

Discrimination training was conducted on the third day and was continued until ten correct responses in twelve consecutive trials within a maximum number of 208 trials were achieved. The average number of trials for Group A was 72 or about six minutes (the intertrial interval was five seconds) and for Group B, 44 trials or less than four minutes. Nine subjects, six assigned to Group A and three to Group B, were unable to learn their respective discrimination tasks in 208 trials; they were replaced by new subjects.

The subjects in Group A achieved considerable success; ten of the fifteen subjects responded correctly on several of the posttest trials. Clearly, discrimination training effected correct learning of the /sr/ response.

(3) *Retention.* Perhaps one of the reasons why retention

of new articulatory associations is so poor is that there is pro-active interference from existing NLH's. Although this hypothesis, as indicated above, has received minimal support from laboratory studies, we made several attempts to test the theory of extraexperimental sources of interference with speech sounds. At least two reasons can be given why speech responses may give positive results where orthographic stimuli and responses have failed. They are as follows: (1) Speech responses should represent the "basic" response level of NLH's, since a written code is usually an inexact representor of a natural language, from which the NLH's are presumed to spring; for example, written word counts may not correspond to spoken word counts, the latter being the assumed source of interference in the above theory. (2) Storage of conflicting responses should follow the oral system rather than the written one; for example, trigram counts that cross syllable boundaries may ill-represent intraunit associations.

At least one reason can be given for the use of children as subjects in preference to adults. The reason is that given and stated by Keppel (1964, p. 77): "research with children may provide information with regard to new or raw learning, that is, learning which may be considered to have occurred for the first time, rather than being based on previously learned mediators or associations. . . . But these mediators must have been acquired at some time in the history of the subject, and research with children may shed some light on this problem."

The general plan of this study was to teach paired associations involving a consonant substitution, which was designed to elicit response interference. The subjects were elementary school children and were taught a list of four pairs by the anticipation method.

An example of the lists, for the experimental and control groups, is as follows:

List 1 (control group) Stimulus—Response		List 2 (experimental group) Stimulus—Response	
○	*vaby*	picture*	*vaby*
✕	*gog*	picture	*gog*
—	*nountain*	picture	*nountain*
▽	*shault*	picture	*shault*

The findings of the several experiments failed to support the assumption that speech sound retention is negatively correlated with associations external to the laboratory situation. Either the design employed here is faulty or the basic theory itself is faulty. However, since PI is a well accepted phenomenon, it seems premature to abandon at this time the concept of extraexperimental interference.

Two segments of the articulatory learning process were considered: response acquisition, the learning of new sounds; and response association, the integration of sounds within grammatical units, such as words. Behavioral processes presumed to operate in each of these two response phases were discussed under the following four headings: (1) transfer, (2) competition, (3) auditory pretraining, and (4) recall.

---

* pictures representing baby, dog, mountain, and salt.

7. THE ROLE OF DISTINCTIVE
FEATURES IN CHILDREN'S
ACQUISITION OF PHONOLOGY*

Paula Menyuk

This investigation studied the acquisition and proportion of correct usage of consonants by Japanese and American children; the consonant substitutions of children developing normal language and of children with articulation problems; and confusion in adults' recall of consonants. A system of distinctive features (gravity, diffuseness, stridency, nasality, continuancy, and voicing) was used to describe the behavior observed.

It was found that features played a hierarchical role in terms of acquisition and proportion of correct usage, as well as in terms of resistance to perceptual and productive confusion. The features also played differing roles depending on the task, the age of the subjects, and their status in learning the sound system of their language.

It has been postulated that the speech sounds of all languages are composed of bundles of features whose parameters are both articulatory and acoustic in nature (Jakobson, Fant, and Halle, 1963). It is the matrix of features

*Reprinted with minor changes from the *Journal of Speech and Hearing Research,* March 1968, Vol. 11.

which differentiates speech sounds from one another by certain attributes. For example, some sounds are differentiated from other sounds in terms of the presence or absence of voicing (/p/ vs. /b/), and then others in terms of the presence or absence of continuancy (/ʃ/ vs. /tʃ/). Some sounds are differentiated from others by a number of attributes involving, for example, nasality, voicing, place, etc. (/m/ vs. /k/). If a comparatively small set of features or attributes can describe the speech sounds in all languages, then, it is hypothesized, these attributes are related to the physiological capacities of man to produce and perceive sounds.

It has also been proposed that, in the child's acquisition of the phonological classes and phonological rules of his language, a regular and valid sequence in the developmental course can be observed (Jakobson, 1962). This sequence is presumably based on the child's increasing capacity to further differentiate speech sounds by the distinctive features of the sounds in a language. For example, at some stage of development, he may distinguish sounds into ± nasal (/b/ vs. /m/ or /d/ vs. /n/) but be unable to distinguish between sounds in terms of place of articulation (/b/ vs. /d/ or /m/ vs. /n/). The actual facts of this developmental course have yet to be obtained although several models of this development have been proposed based on the hypothesis that the direction is from the least marked segments in terms of features to progressively more marked segments. However, we do not have the data to posit a specific order of acquisition of feature distinctions.

Despite the fact that this developmental course has not been carefully analyzed and that there is, in fact, very little research reported on the perceptual distinctions children can make between speech sounds during early childhood (from birth to three years), some data have been collected on the mastery of speech sounds by American children aged two to six (Powers, 1957) and the correct usage of consonants in syllables by Japanese children aged one to three (Nakazima, 1961). Some data have been collected on the sound substitutions made by children, roughly three to seven years, during the developmental period (Menyuk, 1964a), and the substitutions made by children, age three to twelve, with articulation problems. In addition, there are some data on the perceptual confusions of adults (Wicklegren, 1966).

The purpose of this paper is to analyze, in terms of its distinctive feature content, available data concerning correct usage of consonants during the morpheme construction period, the data obtained on the consonant substitutions made by children during the developmental period and those made by children with articulation problems, and the available data on the confusions of adults. It might then be possible to define the order of the acquisition of the attributes of speech sounds and, thus, derive some information about possible cues used in the perception and production of consonants by children during the developmental period rather than merely labeling the process. Further, it might be feasible to derive possible explanations for the order observed in terms of the capacities of the human organism to produce and distinguish speech sounds.

METHOD AND RESULTS

The features investigated in this analysis were gravity, diffuseness, stridency, nasality, continuancy, and voicing. The data on adult consonant substitutions were obtained from the results of an experiment in which subjects were asked to recall a list of syllables composed of consonant plus

/a/. The developmental data were obtained by transcribing the consonant substitutions produced by children while spontaneously generating sentences. The data on children with articulation problems were obtained by transcribing the consonant substitutions produced by children while spontaneously generating sentences (Menyuk, 1964b), and an analysis of the results of the Templin-Darley articulation test (Templin and Darley, 1960) which had been administered to a group of children diagnosed as having articulation problems.

The data on the mastery of consonantal speech sounds were analyzed by determining the percentage of sounds containing a feature that was used correctly at various ages during the developmental period observed. For example, if three out of the ten speech sounds marked + grave in the grammar were correctly used or mastered at age X, then it was noted that there was thirty percent usage of this feature at this age. This same calculation was done for all the features.

Figure 1 shows the rise in percentage of usage of features

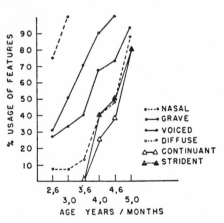

FIGURE 1. Percentage of usage of features in consonants used correctly from age two and a half to five years by American children.

by American children over an age range of two and a half to five years, and indicates the order of mastery of speech sounds containing these features during this period. According to these data complete mastery of the consonant sounds occurs after six + years. Consonant clusters were not included in this analysis.

Figure 2 shows the percentage of usage of features in correct use of consonants in syllables by Japanese children over an age range of one to three years, and indicates the order of correct use of consonants containing these features during this period. It should be noted that the Japanese population was younger than the American population, but that correct production in a syllable rather than mastery in words was being examined.

If we examine the rank order both in terms of time of mastery or correct usage, and percentage of mastery or correct usage at the oldest age sampled, we can observe a striking similarity between Japanese and American children in

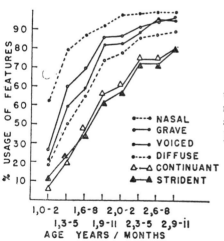

FIGURE 2. Percentage of usage of features in consonants used correctly from age one to three years by Japanese children.

the order of feature acquisition during the developmental periods observed. This is shown in table 1. Both groups of children were proportionately using consonants that contained the features + nasal, + grave, and + voice more correctly and mastering them sooner than those which contained the features + diffuse, + continuant, and + strident.

In the case of American children, where we do have statistics on frequency of consonant usage by adults (Irwin, 1947), these results are largely a contradiction of what is presumably heard in the primary linguistic data. An analysis of the rank order of feature usage as shown in the proportional usage of consonants by English speaking adults is: diffuse, nasal, voiced, continuant, strident, and grave.

TABLE 1. Rank order of use of features as shown in the correct use or mastery of consonants.

Rank Order	Japanese Age 1–3	American Age 2.5–5 years
1	nasal	nasal
2	grave	grave
3	voice	voice
4	diffuse	diffuse
5	continuant	continuant
6	strident	strident

To examine the role of the distinctive features in the consonant substitutions of children acquiring the sound system of their language, and in those acquiring this system in a sufficiently deviant manner to be labeled "articulation problems," and to examine the role of these features in the perceptual confusions of adults, the following procedure was used. All the substitutions observed were analyzed by noting which features were maintained in the substitution.

If, for example, /t/ was substituted for /θ/ as in "tank" for "thank," the following is the analysis that resulted:

	t	θ		t	θ		t	θ
Nasal	—	—	Voice	—	—	Continuant	—	+
Grave	—	—	Diffuse	+	+	Strident	—	—

It could then be noted that all the features were maintained in this substitution except continuancy. The percentage of maintenance of features for all the substitutions in the three groups was then calculated and a rank order of maintenance of features obtained. This rank order for the three groups is given in table 2.

As can be seen in table 2, there are differences between groups in rank order of maintenance of features in substitutions. Stridency is the feature best maintained by adults in their recall of CV syllables, while it is the feature least maintained by the children in the "articulation problem" group in their production of consonants. Voicing and nas-

TABLE 2. Rank order of maintenance of features in consonant substitution.

Rank Order	Adult Recall	Children's Production Developmental	Children's Production Articulation Problem
1	strident	voice	nasal
2	voice	nasal	voice
3	nasal	strident	grave
4	continuant	continuant	continuant
5	grave	grave	diffuse
6	diffuse	diffuse	strident

ality continue to rank high in all groups. In the adult group and the developmental group, gravity and diffuseness rank lowest in feature maintenance while gravity ranks high in the "articulation problem" group.

A chi-square evaluation was used to compare the percentage of maintenance of each feature in the consonant substitutions of the three groups. There are no significant differences between the adults and the children developing language normally in the percentage of maintenance of each feature in substitutions. The children with articulation problems maintain all features significantly less in their consonant substitutions than do children who are developing language normally. The only exceptions are the features ± nasal. In these cases there is no significant difference between the groups. Also the difference is less marked with the features ± grave. These results are shown in table 3.

TABLE 3. Percentage of maintenance of features in consonant substitution.

Feature	Percentage of Adult Recall	Percentage of Children's Production Developmental	P* Value	Percentage of Children's Production Articulation Problem
Voice	85	100	0.01	58
Nasal	85	100		88
Grave	69	50	0.05	29
Strident	88	75	0.01	9
Continuant	75	67	0.01	17
Diffuse	56	50	0.01	13

*P value obtained by chi square evaluation.

DISCUSSION

The results of the above analysis indicate that the distinctive features of the speech sounds of the language that were examined play a differing role in the perception and production of these sounds. One can observe the same order in acquisition and relative degree of mastery or correct usage of sounds containing the various features by groups of children from two differing linguistic environments, indicating that a hierarchy of feature distinction may be a linguistic universal, probably dependent on the developing perceptive and productive capacities of the child. The features that dominate these children's correct usage of consonants at the beginning stages of morpheme construction are + nasal, + grave, and + voice. When we observe the substitutions of adults in recall of consonants, and the consonant substitutions in the productions of children who are developing language normally and those who are not, we observe that the features of voicing and nasality are among the best maintained in these substitutions. One might then postulate that the features ± nasal and ± voice are easiest to perceive, recall, and produce.

± Strident and ± continuant features seem to play a differing role depending on the task, the age of the subject, and his status in the acquisition of the sound system of his language. In recall of consonants by adults, ± strident features are best maintained. Consonants containing + strident and + continuant features are correctly used or mastered last by both Japanese and American children. In the production of consonants by normal speaking children, ± strident features are those best maintained after ± voice and ± nasal features. However, for the children with articulation problems, ± strident features are those least maintained. + Strident, + continuant, and — grave features are very bound up together by virtue of the fact that most consonants marked + strident in grammar are also marked + continuant (the only exceptions are the stops /tʃ/ and /dʒ/) and — grave (the only exceptions are the labio-dentals /f/ and /v/) (Halle, 1961). The sounds /f/ and /v/ are mastered earlier than the other stridents, and the stops /tʃ/ and /dʒ/ are less frequently substituted in the development of the phonological system than their continuant complements, /ʃ/ and /ʒ/. Further, the sounds that are mastered last and most frequently substituted are not — strident but + continuant and — grave (/θ/ and /ð/). It may be that it is not, as has been traditionally assumed, the articulatory gestures used to produce the + strident aspect of a consonant per se (at least for normal speaking children) that makes these consonants late in the developmental scale and difficult to master, but, rather the + continuant and — grave aspects of these sounds.

A possible explanation for this conclusion may be that the other features of consonants which are maintained better and acquired and mastered sooner seem to represent articulatory gestures which have on-off characteristics or a maximal degree of difference. The vocal cords vibrate or they do not (± voice); the sound is emitted through the nasal passages or it is not (± nasal). The attributes + continuant and — grave seem to represent a varying degree of difference. It is on for a somewhat longer time than a burst (+ continuant) and it is produced somewhere other than the periphery of the vocal mechanism (— grave). These statements are merely hypothetical explanatory notions. Much further exploration is needed to isolate the specific parameters of speech stimuli that are easier or more difficult to distinguish and produce.

A feature which also seems to represent a maximal degree of difference is the feature + grave. If a consonant is marked + grave, it is produced at the periphery of the vocal mechanism (i.e., /b/ and /g/). This may account for the fact that consonants marked + grave are used relatively earlier and mastered sooner by both Japanese and American children and that children with articulation problems more frequently maintain the features $\pm$ grave in their substitutions than do the other two groups. The features of place, $\pm$ grave, and $\pm$ diffuse are least maintained in the recall of consonants by adults and in the production substitutions of children acquiring the phonological rules of their language. In this instance we may be observing the results of the statistical occurrences in the language. According to Denes (1963), the most frequent occurrence of minimal pairs in English is from plosives to fricatives ($\pm$ continuant or $\pm$ strident), then from nasals to semi-vowels and liquids ($\pm$ nasal); and then a change in voicing. The most frequent errors in consonant substitution by adults take place among the plosives and the fricatives (an error of place) but not between them. The most frequent errors in consonant substitution by children developing language normally take place among the plosives, fricatives, and semi-vowels and liquids (an error of place) and, in addition, in fewer instances, errors in continuancy occur. The most frequent substitutions in these instances occur between the following sounds: ð/d, θ/t.

One might hypothesize that errors are not usually made between plosives and fricatives, in most instances, because this is a distinction important in the language since it differentiates minimal pairs, whereas errors in place frequently occur since this distinction is not important. In this case knowledge of the language in terms of its minimal-pairs content would be necessary. On the other hand, one might also hypothesize that it is easier to perceive differences between plosives and fricatives than among them and, therefore, the language evolved so that the most frequent occurrence of minimal pairs reflects this greater ease in distinction. Again, this hypothesis needs further exploration through an analysis of the minimal pairs content of other languages and the consonant substitutions of children acquiring these languages.

One further factor should be discussed in terms of the role of distinctive features in children's acquisition of phonology. As was stated, the speech sounds of the language are composed of a bundle of features. They are not only ± a feature. The child, therefore, must in most instances observe several distinctions between speech sounds. As we have noted, distinction between sounds that differ from each other only in one feature (place of articulation) seems to cause the greatest difficulty both in recall by adults and production by children. The one other feature distinction that is frequently not observed is continuancy. The tendency, then, seems to be nonobservation of a single feature differentiation in the most frequent consonant substitutions of the child who is developing language normally. For example, we find substitutions such as "tar" for "car," "dis" for "this," or "fink" for "think." In each of these substitutions all the attributes are maintained except for one in each instance (that is, place, continuancy, stridency).

In the case of children with articulation problems, there are several features that may be nondistinct simultaneously. If we take as an example the case of an eleven-year-old boy with no known physiological factor causing his persistent articulation problem, we observe the following rules in his grammar:

1. All stops that are + grave or — grave become — grave
                 — diffuse + diffuse   + diffuse
                                               + voice

2. All final stops become — voice.

From rule 1 the following morphemes are produced: "dar" for "car," "dirl" for "girl," "die" for "tie," "bidder" for "bigger," "walding" for "walking," and "midden" for "mitten." However, morphemes such as "baby" and "paper" are correctly produced. From rules 1 and 2 the following morphemes are produced: "Bop" for "Bob," "dit" for "did," "doot" for "good," "wat" for "wag," "date" for "cake." Because of the nonobservation of both place and voicing distinctions in his construction of morphemes, this child's speech becomes almost incomprehensible. This was not the result when only one attribute was not being observed as in the consonant substitutions of normal-speaking children. This difference leads us to the question of memory for the various features which distinguish speech sounds, and memory for the use of these features in phonological rules. Comparative studies of substitutions in speech sound components and the use of these components in sequences may elicit information about the effect of possible differences in basic memory capacity to acquire the phonology of the language. Further, they may allow us to more clearly define incomprehensibility in terms of the features that are not observed and in what context.

An attempt has been made to examine several pieces of evidence to determine the role that distinctive features play in the child's acquisition of the sound system of his language, and to relate the results of this examination to some hypotheses about the child's developing perceptual and productive capacities. Through this kind of analysis, possible explanations of the correlations between the primary linguistic data the child hears and how he deals with it at various stages of development may be derived. In this analysis different kinds of data, which have bearing on the processes of phonological acquisition and development, have been lumped together. Further, the role of the distinctive features has been analyzed in a very gross manner in that the use of these features in the phonological rules of children was not examined but only their role in sound acquisition. Therefore, the analysis presented in this paper is quite preliminary. However, the evidence for a more thorough and meaningful analysis is still to be obtained. The major lack, at present, is that no data are available on the perceptual distinctions children make during the developmental period of morpheme construction and on their use of phonological rules during this same period.*

* This work was supported in part by the National Institutes of Health (Grant 5 R01 NB-04332-05) and by the U.S. Air Force Cambridge Research Laboratories, Office of Aerospace Research Contract No. AF19 (628)-5661. Grateful acknowledgment is given to Allan C. Goodman and his staff at the Children's Hospital Medical Center, Boston, Massachusetts, for making available the data on the results of the *Templin-Darley Tests of Articulation*.

COLLOQUIUM

On the afternoon of the second day of the conference, a number of persons from surrounding institutions and schools were invited to meet with the conference participants for the purpose of submitting questions to them and hearing their responses. The audience was composed of speech pathologists, teachers of speech, teachers of English and foreign languages, and students. What follows is a transcript of the impromptu responses of the panel members to the questions submitted. It is preceded by a brief summary of the discussion that had occurred among the panel members during the preceding day and a half.

MINER: On behalf of the entire Department of Speech Correction, I would like to take this opportunity to welcome you to the first annual Lincolnland Conference on Dialectology. Let me begin by introducing the panel to you. Starting with our distinguished lady panel member first, Dr. Paula Menyuk, from the Research Laboratory of Electronics at Massachusetts Institute of Technology. Next, Dr. Marvin Carmony, from the Department of English at Indiana State University. Dr. Carmony is primarily a dialectologist by training. Next to him is Dr. Hurst, from the Office of the Dean at Howard University; he's particularly interested in some of the psychosocial aspects of Negro dialects. Sitting next to Dr. Hurst is Dr. Thomas Shriner, from the Children's Research Center at the University of Illinois. Dr. Shriner's research efforts have focused on aspects of language and most recently on the culturally deprived child. Next to Dr. Shriner is Dr. Harris Winitz, from the Speech and Hearing Department at the University of Missouri in Kansas City. His interest is in the modification of verbal behavior. Next is Dr. James Curtis, Head of the Department of Speech Pathology and Audiology at State University of Iowa. He has some strong interest in the area of experimental phonetics. Lastly, is Dr. Fred Chreist, who is Director of the Speech and Hearing Center at the University of Albuquerque, New Mexico. He's been concerned with dialects as they relate to certain Indian and Spanish-American populations in his region. This gives you, then, a thumbnail sketch of our blue ribbon panel.

As you may know, the panel members have been participating in a professional think time conference for the past 1½ days. I'll attempt to give you a very brief summary of our proceedings to date. I'm sure that the participants here are as interested to hear this summary as anyone because we've had some very spirited discussion. I must be very candid with you at the outset, and say that what I am presenting to you as a summary of our proceedings represents my own thinking. If I were to shift this responsibility to any other panel member, he might interpret our conference differently. Any faults of my presentation I'll claim as my own. Any strengths we will claim as consensus among all of us. I think probably I can best begin by saying that among all the various activities that men encounter everywhere, there seems to be one distinctive feature of the culture, namely, language. Man has a very highly developed language system. He has a mechanism which is capable of producing, storing, retrieving, and transmitting information. Fortunately, we are not all carbon-copy communicators. We tend to have individual differences and these differences exist both between and within speech communities. The evaluation of these differences becomes a real professional problem for speech pathologists. What standards should apply in evaluating speech and language patterns? This is a very complex issue, and I think that it represents a major point of articulation between the fields of dialectology and those individuals interested in disordered communication. There are several significant dimensions to our present meeting. First of all, while there have been other conferences on the subject of dialectology, to our knowledge there has been no conference which has been concerned about the relationship between dialects and speech and language problems. Apparently, the panel members felt also that this represented a dire professional interest area. There seemed to be a void here, because every panel member invited to participate in this conference accepted. We think this was highly significant. In other words, we see that there is a need to establish an interdisciplinary dialogue on the subject of dialects and its relationship to speech and language problems. Now, the conference was conducted in the following manner: each of the participants presented a paper and then we had a considerable amount of discussion and interaction after the presentation of each paper. I will not go into that particular part of it per se, because, as you know, the proceedings of the entire conference are being tape recorded and transcribed, and they will be published soon.

If I can present in capsule form some of the things that

we really got into this morning, in terms of issues and problems and areas of agreement and disagreement, it would go like this. First, we need to distinguish between a dialect (or that which is different) and that which is defective. The two are not necessarily the same. A communication pattern may be just representing a dialect variation, or it may represent something that is totally defective. Consequently, we've got to make a distinction here between what is normal and what is deviant. Secondly, the panel members suggested that we need to dichotomize this notion of deviancy so that we can distinguish variations within speech communities as one part of the dichotomy from the second part, namely, the cross-sectional deviation in speech or language patterns without regard to the particular social status of the individual involved. And this later dimension needs to be again subdivided into the individuals who have the normal capacity for the acquisition of language and those that have restricted or limited capacity for normal acquisition. The panel seemed to be pretty much in consensus that the concept of deviancy needs to be interpreted in terms of certain psychosocial factors, certain speaker-hearer relationships, and in terms of the different rules for generating grammar, both within and between dialects. We further went on to discuss the notion that future research in this area should be directed to the acquisition of dialects. There are many unanswered questions in this area which we need to identify. One key question which was raised was this: "How do we describe the acquisition of grammar within dialects?" We have available procedures to begin this kind of analysis. It's a researchable question and certainly much research effort needs to be directed in this area of the acquisition of dialects. Secondly, we raised a very serious question about the relationship between linguistic development and cognitive development, both within and between dialects. We're suggesting here that it's not only language but how man uses it which represents an important area needing further exploration. Finally, we did come up with one statement, which I think may be particularly useful to public school speech therapists: When speech pathologists are dealing with misarticulations, they are interested in speech production, defective allophones. However, most dialectic pronunciation errors are a matter of the distribution of the phonemes, not defective allophones. This was essentially Dr. Carmony's notion, and perhaps he would wish to pursue this further.

In a very telescopic fashion, this represents some of the proceedings that have transpired during the past day and a half. Let's turn now to some questions and answers. I'd like to toss the conversational ball down to Dr. Chreist and ask him to read his first question and give us his reaction.

CHREIST: I don't know whether I was elected to be first speaker because I came from the greatest distance or because this question was most controversial as far as one of our discussions from this morning. The question is: "What is a sound working position for now toward dialects which may be taken by the speech correctionist?" Many of you that are in our audience today are working in the field and this question comes to you. The population is present. You have someone who refers a child or an adult to you as a speech correctionist and your question is: "What should I do with this individual?" In our discussion there were various opinions which were stated, and I am giving my personal opinion from this point of view as a former speech pathologist in a public school system, ten years in South Bend, Indiana, and as a director of a clinic for twenty years at the University of New Mexico. I feel that the job of the speech correctionist is very much involved with this problem. The problem is there; therefore, you have to do something about it. First, you must determine whether it is a clinically, educationally significant problem. This goes back to our discussion of whether it's a case of defective allophones or the distribution of allophones. I see this in terms of what I consider "Differential Diagnosis," one of the major jobs of a speech correctionist. That is, it is the job of determining on the basis of the acoustic symptom that is presented to you by this child, what you feel as a beginning point is the particular problem. On the basis of the training you have had, I feel it is your job then to determine whether you and your staff are capable of handling this specialized problem or whether it needs to be referred to another area. What are some of these symptoms which we will be evaluating? Well, certainly there are the symptoms at the phonological level, as far as dialect problems are concerned. There are problems at the morphological and syntactical level. There are problems at the structural level which will appear at certain times as symptoms in which they are being misused or rearranged by the client you are evaluating. Last of all, there are certain semantic differences and problems that will occur. Now, from the training that most speech pathologists have had, I contend that you are capable of making this kind of a differential diagnosis at the surface level. When it comes to the deep level, you will need the assistance of other specialists in the field. Note that I have eliminated social implications, the psychological implications of the conclusions you may draw from your initial evaluation. I feel it is a place to begin and your first job is to make this kind of a differential diagnosis, and say I have a dialect problem. It may be, as we derived from our discussion, a continuum of conditions. At one end a simple local sound substitution and at the other end what I call, and will continue to call, foreign accent. Because as I define the foreign accent, it's an evaluation by the hearer on the basis of his native language background. His perception of the speech which is produced causes him to say, "This is foreign to me." Now, don't misunderstand by the word foreign, I do not mean that as a derogatory implication. I mean that it is not within his pattern or your pattern as a speech clinician of the native language which you speak. Therefore, I feel that the speech pathologist or the speech correctionist has the initial job of making the differential diagnosis. From there, then, we move into the decision of whether some kind of therapy or corrective program should be undertaken.

MINER: At this point, let's turn to Dr. Winitz.

WINITZ: My question reads: "In light of your interest in learning theory principles, if Eliza Doolittle came to you, what would you do that professor Henry Higgins did not do?" First, I would check my ASHA Certification records and if I am adequately certified, I would then accept the client. Essentially, his approach was a matching-the-sample approach; stimulus, response, reinforcement, try it again, try again, try it again. This is a principle of learning theory. Repetition or frequency is critical in any aspect or task. In any learning task, one often evaluates the growth curves in terms of the number of trials, on the assumption that learning is a function of the number of trials. There are other procedures, however, that one might use. One which has, I think, considerable potential but has not been highly developed is one which I call segmentation of the learning phase. And one can segment this in a variety of ways using any one of a number of theoretical schemes. The approach can be demonstrated as follows. Let's assume you are teaching a child or an adult (and this can be done rather rapidly) the velar back-sound which is often heard in Hebrew or

Arabic. How does one teach this particular sound? First, one takes a look at its distinctive features, using one of a number of systems. Then one ascertains a response that is available to the subject. Most people can snore and so this is a good place to start to teach the subject to make an inspirated sound. When the subject has mastered this particular element, he moves on to inspiration, expiration, ingressive, regressive, and, finally, you want to eliminate the inspirated sound. There are a number of principles involved in this sequence and they are behavioral principles primarily. You start with the available response. You move at a rate which maintains a physiological positioning, a posturing. I found that if I wait ten or twenty seconds and ask the subject to go from the snore sound to the velar sound, he loses this muscular sense and he's unable to proceed. So the procedure here is to move rather rapidly, approximately at five-second intervals, because my machine is programmed in this way. I thought if I were doing it, I would move more rapidly than that. Move from one discrete unit to the next. This is one approach, and this is a production approach. Essentially, one of teaching a response that is not available to the subject.

MINER: Here's a question which I'll direct to Dr. Carmony. It says, "How do you define Speech Community?"

CARMONY: In terms of a high density of communication. This is a relative matter, of course.

MINER: What do you mean?

CARMONY: Well, I mean where there is a very great deal of communicating. This is one aspect of what constitutes speech community. Another aspect of it would be to say that a speech community exists where the idiolects, that is the individual speech patterns, have a high proportion of shared features. So, it's still relative.

MINER: As long as we're on that end of the table, let's move next to Dr. Hurst and ask him to read and react to his question.

HURST: "Some linguists contend that current research on Negro dialects focuses only on pedagogically trivial problems such as minor sound pattern differences, usually in the rubric of dialectolalia and ignore the all important problems of differences in underlying grammatical rules. What is your reaction to this charge?" No, I think that this is not true. There may be some few people who are engaging initially in research in this area and either did not have the interest in going further or have not had the sophistication to recognize the true dimensions of them. In actuality, those of us who've been working in Washington with the problem are concerned with all the components of linguistics or we might even say psycholinguistic behavior, morphology, syntax, phonology, semantics, perception of self, role impact of environment and experience on cognitive and linguistic development. All of this with a view toward deriving effective measures for helping persons cope with the demands made upon them by the educational, economic, and social circumstances in which they find themselves. I think that the most effective research in the future will come out of the realization that the most serious results of being poor and/or living in relative social isolation in this country, occur in the area of cognitive function in general, in processes of thinking and in language skills, including reading. I think it's generally understood that children from rural, urban, or rural slums (some might want to contest what I mean by rural slums, but I'm rapidly coming to the conclusion that this is the only definition that's suitable to me) are apt to have linguistic deviations in the areas of articulation, vocabulary, grammar, etc. And these are important, but school

and other records also indicate, I think, an irrevocably in-
terrelated involvement with their limited capacity in such
things as observing and stating sequences of events, processing information, perceiving cause and effect relationships,
grouping concrete phenomena into classes of phenomena,
and this could go on for quite some time. Certainly, if a
child's sensory discrimination, language, and cognitive
skills are inadequately developed, he's going to have trouble
in school. He's going to have problems coping with these
varied demands of the environment. My own purpose in
working in this area of so-called Negro dialect is to develop
an individual who is a better functioning individual, and
because language is so essential to adequate functioning in
social, educational, or economic circumstances, then this is
where I feel I should put my own personal emphasis.

SHRINER: I'd like to add a little to what Dr. Hurst is saying in the sense that my question is, "When are different
speech and language patterns defective?" This is relevant
to what he was saying, because one of the things we talked
about in the conference was the concept of two different
codes, Code 1 and Code 2. Code 1 refers to a local dialect
pattern which would be related to a specific area within a
speech community. Code 2 refers to a group with its own
sort of grammatical structures which could exist at the syntactical level, semantic level, etc. Code 1 or group 1 consists
of a local dialect group with speech variations functioning
primarily at the phonological level, and making the assumption that there are no associated syntactical problems. In
Dr. Hurst's question, the concept of dialectolalia was concerned specifically with the sort of minute deviations of
speech patterns, tiny phonological differences which would
be primarily related to our local dialect group patterns or
patterns within a speech boundary. I suggested in my paper

at the conference that we adopt a larger framework or method for looking at language per se which would be related to our Code 2 group. This is the group that Dr. Hurst is also concerned with and this is where the socially disadvantaged child, or more formally the culturally disadvantaged child, has his problems. One of the outcomes of the conference was this: if we get a culturally disadvantaged child, or a child with many of the psychosocial problems that are involved in his particular speech community patterns, we should work on language per se, language in the sense of the broad definition of language, including problem-solving tasks, and cognitive abilities. After we have gone through our Code 2 with him and made significant gains, then we can refer him to Code 1. But now the question comes up, "Who does this?" Is the speech pathologist trained to work with Code 2 patterns or is the speech pathologist only concerned with the Code 1 type of patterns, the local dialect patterns? The speech therapist is traditionally concerned with articulation patterns. If we adopt the larger viewpoint, this would require some changes in our curriculum, the way we teach our graduate students, etc. We would need to adopt the framework of a speech-language clinician, someone who would be trained in the area of not only working primarily with the Code 1 problem, the local or regional dialect pattern, but also working on the language pattern to get the child to Code 1 if speech therapy is recommended. In other words, what I'm trying to say is that the problem of dialectolalia would be primarily the responsibility of the speech clinician. However, if we do get a child that does walk into our clinic and this child has other associated problems, what do we do? We have to call upon other specialists, other people trained in child development, child psychology, other referrals that help us with our problems. We are only one member of what is probably a small team. I think that we could make, as Dr. Chreist has suggested, a larger contribution to this problem if we are willing to accept our responsibility. Dr. Curtis suggested this morning that maybe we wouldn't want to start training our people in second language learning. This is like teaching a second language. Are we individuals who should be responsible for teaching a second language?

HURST: There's one point I wanted to speak to that's implicit in the question raised with me, and it has to do with the term "Negro dialect." This is a term that I feel should be handled with great sensitivity, if it is used at all. It seems to create so many needless problems, problems that we just can't afford to waste an awful lot of time with. I would prefer to see it avoided altogether, and I'd like to see the description of the problem worded in more detail so that we both know what we are talking about and could proceed from there. I'm afraid that simple utilization of the term Negro dialect leaves a great deal unsaid, leaves a great deal dependent upon the interpretation of the listener and, as a result, a great deal of miscommunication takes place. In addition to this, it seems to me that there is a disruptive potential psychologically, in view of the many social problems that we know exist in this country.

MINER: We've gone entirely too long without hearing from the woman representative on our panel, let's see what Dr. Menyuk has to say:

MENYUK: "Are there differences in syntactic structures, or semantic fields between the normal and the culturally disadvantaged child? Please elaborate." The answer to that question is, you cannot answer it in terms of the whole. I think some of this is being implied today. Cultural disadvantageousness occurs throughout this country, in various areas of the country. Whether or not within a given community, that is so-called culturally deprived or disadvantaged, where a particular language system deviates from some kind of standard in terms of syntactic structure or semantic field is something that we must address ourselves to. It is an empirical question and we must then see if it is always the case that cultural disadvantageousness leads to a differentiation in linguistic systems. Outside of that rather general statement I would like to say that the given linguistic systems that have been looked at, at least in the literature, lead one to believe that there are differences in the system. But let me describe what I mean by differences in the system. Let us say, for example, that language is made up of universals. It is important for us to be able to express in language certain functional relationships, like what is this subject, and what is the object. We must be able to pluralize; we must be able to express tense. If you look at the very, very slender data that are available, again in those linguistic communities that have been looked at, what you find is not that these universals are missing from the language of this particular community. On the contrary, you may find variations that don't even exist in the standard language, gradations that are the result of a particular culture. But, they are there. The only difference is in the ways in which this is resolved in a particular language. For example, look at William Stewart's data on Negro dialects in the Baltimore area. He finds that, for example, although we may talk about a present and a past, a present progressive and a past progressive, one finds in this particular linguistic system three variations between present, progressive, past progressive. There are three degrees of variation with their own unique marking. Consequently, you find a child saying, "I be's good, I being good, etc." Now we listen to this and we say it's different and it is, because we don't mark tense in this way. But this child has acquired the rules that exist in his community for marking tense. So that, although they are differences, they are not missing. Whether this holds throughout every linguistic culturally disadvantaged community that we look at is again an empirical question. The data thus far lead us to believe that; although, like in different languages, one may resolve these linguistic universals in a different way and that these linguistic universals exist in those systems. Now, semantic fields, this to me is an area that is extremely interesting and the data are extremely sparse. People have collected vocabulary items so that you can, for example, look at significant differences in mean number of words that are used per utterance for a sample time or something like this. But nobody has done an analysis of the semantic property of these lexical items and to me this would be a very interesting kind of thing to do. For example, do you find single lexical items used in a particular linguistic system in many different ways so that exclusion or differentiation is not taking place? Do you find in other instances different lexical items being used only specifically when they should be used generally? In other words is there overgeneralization, is there undergeneralization in the use of lexical items? Again this is an empirical question. And then, of course, as far as semantic fields are concerned, do we find lexical items existing in these communities that don't exist at all in other communities? Do they have standard meanings in one community? All these questions are in front of us and remain to be resolved.

CURTIS: One of the questions put in front of me here, and which I'd like to respond to a little bit, but perhaps in a little larger context than the question itself as stated here and then relate it to some of the other things the panel has said. Let me read the question. "If some type of management or changing of dialects should be done in the schools, when should it be done by the speech correctionist, by the classroom teacher, by the public-speaking teacher, or others?" Well now, there's a lot in that question and I don't want to report too long. In the first place, I think a person asking such a question must have some kind of assumption as to what he means by dialect. And I think coming out of our discussions yesterday and today has been some focusing on the fact that there can be a number of different kinds of things implied by the term dialect. They can extend from differences which are obvious, most obvious perhaps in hearing somebody talk, but differences in the language that had been acquired by an individual of sufficient magnitude and in enough different dimensions so that one can probably only properly think of this as actually constituting a different language. An individual may have no problem so long as he is in contact with the people with whom he needs to communicate in the language community in which he grew up. It's only when he attempts to move outside this community, and to deal with other people that he begins to have a problem. He has grown up in a language community and developed a competence in relationship to a language. He may eventually move and be looked upon as having a nonstandard kind of language. Now in trying to communicate with this larger community, he finds himself handicapped. But what he needs is not simply a little correction of some defects in the language he's acquired; essentially what he needs to do, as somebody put it earlier, is to acquire new tools, which in this case really means learning the second language. I think the real question is, if to those instances where this kind of description is apt and appropriately applied, assuming that there are such individuals, to determine whether this description is correct and with respect to how many people it's correct, and what are the dimensions of the difference along which we need to consider such instances. But to the extent that it can be considered to be a reasonable characterization of the problem of some individuals, and I think we can really raise the question as to whether or not we in fact have any of these people who were appropriately provided with the preparation in their college education or graduate educations to deal with this problem. I think it's an appropriate question to ask whether the speech correctionist, the classroom teacher, the public-speaking teacher, or any such individual has been provided with the tools and knowledge, skills, clinical judgment, and insight that might be necessary to deal with these problems. I would assume that probably there are some competencies that each of these individuals has that could be useful in this problem, but whether we have at this stage and time developed a person who has the special knowledge and skill with this kind of problem, I think, is very questionable. In my own judgment, I would say that my answer would be no. Now that does not mean, I think, that everybody has to throw up his hands and say that nothing can be done to help this individual, but I think that it certainly means that people who are attempting to help this individual should be highly conscious of their own limitations in doing so and should not presume to be doing more than they are really competent to do and should be thoroughly aware of the fact that what they are doing is probably only a limited attack on the problem. Now there are other things that are subsumed under the term dialectology which are sometimes of a different character, almost on a different set of dimensions, and for those I think the problem is somewhat different.

MINER: Well we have a very logical transition here down to Dr. Carmony. I believe you have a question which concerns the kinds of training in linguistics a speech correctionist needs or something to that effect, don't you?

CARMONY: Yes, I have. The question reads "What kinds of training in linguistics does the speech correctionist need in order to evaluate and manage dialect problems?" Now, if by dialect problems one is simply talking about matters of selection or incidence of a given sound phoneme, and not matters of defective production of a given sound, then I suppose it would be, and this is a distinction I think we were making, I think it would be valuable for a speech correctionist to perhaps have even as much as an English language and linguistics minor. How he could manage it with everything else he has to do, I don't know. But, it would seem valuable to have a course in general linguistics, just the elements of general linguistics; and, by the way, that's my own background. I think that the speech correctionist should be exposed to consideration of the regional and social variations of the country as a whole, and such consideration [should] constitute a part of some course. Occasionally a good course in the history of the English language will deal with these problems to some extent. I think it would be a fine elective course for speech correctionists. One wouldn't encounter this in a course, but I think that the speech correctionist certainly needs information about the linguistic correlates of the social stratification in his own community. If he has a little training he can do something about this himself. But, I think that he doesn't have any business attempting to get people to pronounce the three (r) 's with three different phones if this isn't the standard pronunciation in the community in which he's teaching, never mind what his own speech pattern is. I mean that. In Terre Haute

I think there are a few people who attempt to get students to say Mary, Mary, Mary (different vowels) when it's just perfectly natural for everybody to say Mary. I think a person would have to know something about, must indeed know something about, regional and social variations in the country as a whole and in his own community. These are the kinds of information we need.

MINER: Dr. Menyuk, I believe you have a couple of questions?

MENYUK: "In consideration and differentiating between linguistic competence and linguistic performance, you further differentiate linguistic capacity. Please explain or elaborate." Take for example two children. One is completely physiologically intact. Presumably he has the capacity to acquire language in the normal way and he proceeds to do that. At various stages of development he essentially has a certain competence in the language, he can do certain things in the language at this stage of development and at later stages of development he would begin to do other things, and at still some later stages of development, toward some asymptote which we have not defined and in some areas they are undefinable, like lexical apposition. Essentially, this competence changes. Now at some stage of development, certain aspects of the grammar are acquired like, for example, the basic structures in syntax are presumably acquired around age four. He can do all kinds of operations with sentences. By that age it is necessary for him to do so. On the other hand, he cannot elaborate, he can't perform elaboration kinds of operations. So one talks about competence in terms of level of acquisition. For example, the child who is not an intact organism, in some way, and I don't want to put it in the nervous system per se, or I must admit I am prejudiced in this direction. Let us say that for some reason you do not have an intact organism. He does not then have the capacity to acquire the kind of competence in language that you observe with the intact organism, and this is the differentiation.

MINER: Dr. Chreist, we haven't heard from you for a while.

CHREIST: Well, the other general question that I had is: "How should you distinguish between differences between dialect groups and substandard speech or language patterns within dialect groups?" I think this was partially answered by Dr. Carmony when he began outlining the various areas. However, if you're dealing with the representative phonological differences, then you are going to be considering the sound structure of the language with the distribution of the sounds in this particular pattern—both that which is "normal" to the dialect group, and accepted by the entire dialect group, and that which is "abnormal." Now the degree of abnormalcy will depend on a number of things and once again I go back again to the speech clinician's basis, the number of sound substitutions and the number of sound distortions, the number of additions and omissions which will be included or excluded in this particular pattern. Now in some dialects certain dialect groups use patterns such as Dr. Carmony's discussions of the Terre Haute Dialect groups, those found in the linguistic atlas as it studies the various areas of the country. Here we have distinguishing features between dialects. Then when you move into the second section of this question, substandard speech or language patterns, within dialect groups, now you're making a value judgment. The basis of this value judgment must be something on a scale of importance and I would use the scale of importance, "Does it interfere with communication, and to what degree does it interfere with communication?" All right, let's move to the next step and say, "Does it cause this person to be maladjusted as far as adjustment to the communication situation?" Once again we are dealing only with the surface phonological level of this particular aspect. However, here the substandard is a value judgment within that community. How deep you go in this value judgment will depend on how damaging it is in terms of the psychosocial ideas that have been presented by other members of the panel.

SHRINER: I'd like to add one small point to the discussion. Dialect patterns are, in my opinion, predominantly vowel patterns; that is, some changes in vowel, and also, in all probability, changes in inflection and intonation. Most speech therapists usually don't do vowel therapy in the strict sense of the word or intonation or inflection therapy.

CHREIST: I don't know if I would agree with that generalization, Dr. Shriner, that most dialect patterns involve vowel changes.

SHRINER: But one thing about my own personal experience. I have a southwestern Pennsylvania dialect superimposed on Iowa-Illinois dialect.

CHREIST: I think it's the first type that was investigated when we were discussing that this morning. I felt, isn't this the reason that this has been consistent in the pattern of investigation as far as the linguistic atlas is concerned? It's the place where they started years ago and I think maybe that now is the time to look more carefully at the consonantal variations.

CARMONY: I don't believe there are really very many regional variations in the consonants. There are certainly regional variations in the distribution of the consonants; now this comes under the heading of selection and incidence.

CHREIST: Would you consider the omission of the [r] an example of a regional consonantal variation?

CARMONY: Well, you could consider this a matter of the incidence of the [r]. So it's a matter of whether it's there or whether it's not. There are areas certainly where having it is disadvantageous and other areas where not having it is certainly disadvantageous. What's normal in deep southern Illinois is very often substandard in Charleston in terms of the incidence of some vowels and even of consonants.

HURST: My next question is: "Please elaborate on differences between culturally disadvantaged, economically disadvantaged, and socially disadvantaged." Since this is a loaded question, I'll answer it. Well, beginning with economically disadvantaged, "When you 'ain't' got no money, you're in trouble." And to extend that, when you don't have marketable skills that will help you get your hands on what is commonly known among the disadvantaged as "Loot" then you are further disadvantaged economically. Now we could continue in that vein. You are culturally disadvantaged when you go to a place like Vietnam, as a representative of this country, and don't know anything about the things that are valued in that country, the history, background, and the people in that country. When you go into the ghettos and slums of New York, Chicago, and so on and you don't know anything about what's happening there, then you are culturally disadvantaged. You have my sympathy. Socially disadvantaged is when you simply don't know how to act in good company. So here again if you are in the proximity of a group of people whose standards of acceptable social behavior are different from what you have been accustomed to, then you are definitely operating at a disadvantage. I have taken sort of a unique way, I think, of answering your question. I hope that the implications are quite clear. Another question is: "Have recent reports on experimental research in applied language or speech and language improvement revealed any common denominators regarding appropriate therapy steps for modification of dialects?" I think that the better person to answer this is probably Dr. Winitz. I think that there are a number of common denominators that are just beyond the grasp of our fingertips. When we have developed the expertise and the sophistication to recognize what they are, then we will be able to answer your question in a more meaningful way. However there are two very significant developments that were impressive to me and that I plan to pursue further after I have had a chance to orient myself so that I won't embarrass myself by the kinds of questions that I ask. The first has to do with the work that is being done by Dr. Menyuk on distinctive features. I think this is very relevant to some of the programs that are being attempted now in terms of being able to evaluate their merit. You see, we're doing some things now that I think are effective and we don't know why. Since we don't know why, we don't know how to continue to refine the programs or the proper directions to take in continuing to refine the programs. Some of the things that Dr. Menyuk said are in connection with distinctive features, as is some of the work that has been completed by Dr. Winitz. I think their work has direct application for some of the problems that you have now. So I would like to toss this idea to them.

WINITZ: We, in our laboratory, have primarily manipulated responses that are considered phonetic or phonemic or some characterization of this particular level of language. I think one can, when one uses rather precise procedures to make gains, be more efficient in his approaches to the problem of articulation learning. I don't think we have time, nor is it appropriate perhaps, to attempt a formulation of some of our problems and how we have attempted to solve them. I think when one looks at the manipulation of behavior, especially language behavior, everyone has to take into account the total language system, however characterized. In addition one must take into account the physiological limitations. Also, one must take into account the acoustic aspects of the speech wave. At the present time, language training, that is, responses that are traditionally considered morphemic or syntactical, cause more difficulty. One can, for example, teach children to say words. Children who have no words can learn words using procedures developed by psychologists who are usually called operant conditioners. People of this professional discipline have studied the problem more than other groups. But the problem of teaching sentences is much more complex. Let's assume that we wanted to teach a child to expand from a single-word utterance to a two-word utterance or to a three-word utterance. I don't know of anyone who can give us information as to how one might do this other than providing a child with a stimulation situation. When I first got interested in attempting to use linguistic models for teaching grammatical structure to children, I felt this was very exciting and I recall that in the early days of my training we simply referred to language training clinics as stimulation clinics. It seems that stimulation is revisited in the sense that even though we have some rather highly developed characterizations, presumably of what might account for well-formed structures, no one has yet laid down the rules or given us a manual as to how one would string utterances together in any fashion. I think this could be done, but I've never attempted to investigate this problem. It does not develop simply by changing one word to the next word. This would almost be impossible. You can do this with a very limited number of utterances but soon one has to utilize some kind of rule formation or concept formation task to teach the child to do this.

MINER: I'm wondering if we couldn't take an implication from this question and perhaps ask both Dr. Curtis and Dr. Menyuk if they'd care to address themselves to some of the therapeutic implications of distinctive feature analysis.

CURTIS: In the paper that I submitted to this conference, I raised the basic question of what is the process of segmentation that needs to be done in the best order to give us an understanding of speech. Now let me see if I can make my terms a little clear here. When I talk about the stream of speech, we are confronted with something that we can view either acoustically as a more or less continuous time series of sound waves which vary more or less continuously all the time or with what I think is a relatively simple transform of that, namely, the physiological events which also go on more or less continuously as we talk without very much interruption. As we normally view this, we describe it in phonological terms and phonetic terms, we break this up into something that we typically view as a string of discrete units. And one view of this is what one may characterize as a linear sequence of the discrete units. It seems to me that we make assumptions when we do this. We assume that these units are, in fact, independent, that they have an integrity of and by themselves. That they are commutable in the sense that we can lift one out and replace it with another one without doing violence to the ones that come before and after. This is implicit in a great deal of talk that's been going on here this afternoon. Dr. Winitz was talking about using certain experimental learning paradigms for teaching particular sounds. He didn't define what he meant

by a sound except by example in one case when he talked
about the [ç] sound. There has been a good deal of talk
about the phone-size or phoneme-size units of speech. We've
all learned to do a phonetic transcription in which we attempt to break up this stream into such discrete units. In
effect we are trying to transform something that is continuous into something that is discrete because we have a
model that says it can be best described as a series of discrete things. Not only do we try to do that, then we try to
take this model and operate on behavior as though these
things were in fact discrete. All I know about the physiological aspects of the behavior says that they're continuous.
You cannot produce a consonant phoneme by itself except
insofar as you can make it a syllable nucleus. The smallest
unit you can possibly produce is a syllable. I was interested
in Dr. Carmony's paper describing some of the dialect characteristics of Terre Haute and to find that his description
of some of the variants that he found in certain vowels had
to be described in terms of their relationships to the phonetic context in which they occurred. They were described in
relationship to particular consonants. They could not really be dealt with as units which were completely separable
and could be taken completely out of context and dealt
with that way. Speech correction has taken this model very
literally and they have done a great many things. They have
dealt with attempting to diagnose or to describe the aberrant or defective speech behavior in terms of what we call
speech sounds or phone-sized units or whatever they call it.
We've attempted to decide what ought to be done about
people's speech in terms of trying to replace such size of
units with other units that we like better. We don't like
these particular ones that the individual has so we're going
to somehow lift those out and replace them with something

else. I'm not sure that this is the most apt and most illuminating model of the behavior and in fact I have rather grave doubts that it is the best kind of way to think about this and the best sort of behavioral unit with which to try to deal. If one is going to try to change speech production behavior, I'm inclined to think that someday we may know enough to be able to specify it better, the kind of unit to try to work with, our thinking about the model to try to work with in developing speech skills and so on. Now one possible such unit is something that we might call distinctive features. I would prefer to use the term articulatory parameters because I want to give the subphonemic features. I am thinking of a clear articulatory reference, a speech production reference. I think the more commonly used systems of distinctive features have other references in addition to this.

I've been interested in some of the experiments that Dr. Winitz and his group have been doing which seem to me to be useful in helping to define some of the kinds of relationships that one needs to have in mind as he possibly develops some techniques for changing behavior. He's been using a type of paradigm that has been developed in the experimental psychology laboratories for certain types of learning experiments. Does he mean to imply that this paradigm which he uses in the laboratory in order to control certain kinds of behavior and to keep certain variables separated ought to be followed in actual clinical procedures of some kind? Would you extrapolate these paradigms as clinical procedures in addition to being laboratory procedures?

WINITZ: Yes, certainly.

CURTIS: Why?

WINITZ: Because I presume that these procedures enable us to more efficiently teach a particular response.

HURST: Sure, these procedures have demonstrated their ability to change behavior. I think that research has demonstrated very ably that we can. We have the tools or the beginnings of methodologies for changing deeply ingrained behaviors and at the very least this gives us a direction in which to go to engage in more research of the same kind or research resulting directly from this activity.

MENYUK: I don't want to go into a long discussion about operant conditioning or mediation or anything like this. However, you can change behavior in a laboratory situation. There is no question about this. You can change it with positive reinforcement or you can change it with negative reinforcement. You can manipulate the response in terms of scheduled reinforcement. The real question, of course, is what does this have to do with the acquisition of unique responses that you would like the child to incorporate into his language system. That is, again, an empirical question which we have to research. But the question I thought you were addressing yourself to was not so much just simply concerned with the phonology, especially when you deal with dialects. Perhaps the ones that we are most interested in are not the ones who are simply concerned with phonology. We are interested in involvements with the whole system across the board. What methods and procedures are to be used in these instances? Also, what methods and procedures should be used with the child who has displayed the fact that he has the capacity to acquire language by going ahead and doing it? We don't have any correct answers to this kind of question. If you look at normal acquisition and development we have a lot of questions about what actually happens in this child-mother interaction situation. We can specifically say that the mother is not tutorial in the sense that she doesn't give you systematic contrasts, which sort of leads to a final concept. She may occasionally say, "Don't say that, say this," and then randomly say something else. Somehow or other this child pieces together this essentially very noisy learning condition and then develops this kind of system and you want to take this other child and you want him to acquire another kind of system involving the syntax, semantics, and phonology. We don't understand really what goes on essentially. The philosophy that is being followed now in many programs that involve fully competent kids, if you will, is to expose them, if you will, to stimulate them. There are a great deal of problems involved in this. They are constantly evaluating. They use I.Q. measures, standards, and scores.

HURST: Would you agree that there are two different levels involved? We are talking about two different kinds of phenomena when we refer to the young child, the developing child, and to the young adult. I'm referring to the difference in the nature of the problem when we are referring to the developing child as compared with the already developed young adult such as the kind you would encounter in your Job Corps speech and hearing center. This is a different kind of problem.

MENYUK: Now we're talking about a grown-up organism and I really don't understand a grown-up organism very well. Essentially, as far as this is concerned, it depends on what you want to change. Is it simply that you want him to acquire a new sound system?

LADY FROM JOB CORPS: No, this is not it at all and the past two years the brainstorm that I have gotten through my work with the Job Corps, and the only thing that I found true with the youngsters of sixteen through twenty-two years of age is that I must simply tell him that in order for him to play a certain role, to be a certain person, namely a person out in the work world, so to speak, the language that you have or your speech just won't do. We just want to show you another one. In other words, we are doing role-changing and what we do in the speech and language center is set up and create new role situations and really can't replace the role. This is the only thing he accepts. He doesn't accept, "I need to change, I'm not right." It's just that someone out there has a dollar that I want to make. If I want that dollar, I must play according to his rules.

MENYUK: It seems to me that perhaps teaching a second language and some of the new techniques that have developed there might be most appropriate. I refer to somebody who is at Northwestern, Ray Moore, whom you might get in touch with, who has been teaching Swahili to Northwestern students who are going out into the Peace Corps because they also are, you know, motivated to acquire a second language.

MINER: I think we probably have reached the point where it's time to draw this conference to a close. I think we can safely say now that we have made some serious attempts to establish our interdisciplinary dialogue concerning the relationship between dialect and speech problems and we leave you with the charge to continue it.

REFERENCES

Introduction

1. Frank F. Miles, "Some Correlates of Two Important Dysla-
   lias," *ASHA, Journal of the American Speech and Hearing
   Association,* vol. 5, no. 7: July, 1963, p. 671.

Chapter 1

1. George L. Trager and Henry Lee Smith, Jr., *An Outline of
   English Structure,* Studies in Linguistics: Occasional Papers, no. 3, 5th printing (Washington, 1957), pp. 11–29.
2. Morris Halle, "Phonology in Generative Grammar," *Word*
   18 (1962) : 54–72. See also J. A. Fodor and J. J. Katz, *The
   Structure of Language: Readings in the Philosophy of Language* (Englewood Cliffs, N. J., 1964), pp. 324–33. See also
   Noam Chomsky and Morris Halle, "Some Controversial
   Questions in Phonological Theory," *Journal of Linguistics*
   1 (1965) : pp. 97–138.
3. "Breaking, Umlaut, and the Southern Drawl," *Language* 42
   (1966) : pp. 18–41.
4. For a good introduction, see Raven I. McDavid, Jr., "The
   Dialects of American English," in Nelson Francis, *The*

Structure of American English (New York: Ronald Press, 1958), pp. 480–543.

5. Marvin D. Carmony, "The Speech of Terre Haute: A Hoosier Dialect Study," Ph.D. dissertation, Indiana University, 1965.

6. Hans Kurath and Raven I. McDavid, Jr., *The Pronunciation of English in the Atlantic States,* University of Michigan Studies in English, No. 3 (Ann Arbor, 1961).

7. Charles F. Hockett, *A Course in Modern Linguistics* (New York: Macmillan Company, 1958), p. 17.

8. See Roman Jakobson, Gunnar M. Fant, and Morris Halle, *Preliminaries to Speech Analysis: The Distinctive Features and their Correlates,* 2nd printing with addition (Cambridge: M.I.T. Press, 1963).

9. The tensing of lax [æ] in *half, path,* and *grass,* mentioned by Sledd (p. 36), occurs in the speech of Brazil, Indiana, fifteen miles east of Terre Haute.

10. [ɚ], the vowel of *further,* is here, taken to be phonemic [ʌr] in stressed syllables, [ər] in unstressed syllables; but see Sledd, pp. 19–25. See also Kurath and McDavid, p. 103.

11. Paralleling pronunciations of *he'll* and *she'll* as *hill* and *shill* are fairly frequent pronunciations of *they'll* as [ðɛχ].

12. Jakobson et al., pp. 29–30.

13. In connected speech, the loss of the second element of the diphthong is common in the pronunciation of *our.* The loss of the offglide also occurs before [l] in the pronunciation of such words as *foul.* One interesting feature of Southern Indiana speech is the occasional use of [æ u] in the stressed syllable of *finally.*

14. Sledd, p. 30.

15. Ibid., p. 31. *Garlic* seems to have only [ɪ] or [i]. *Stomach* may have [ə], [ɨ*], [ɪ], [e], or [i].

Chapter 2

Amstern, H. *Development of Concept Formation in Children.* Berkeley: University of California Press, 1966.

* Preferred phonetic symbol not available.

Bosma, J. F. *Symposium on Oral Sensation.* Springfield, Ill.: Charles C. Thomas, Publisher, 1967.

Bourne, L. E. *Human Conceptual Behavior.* Boston: Allyn and Bacon, 1966.

Chomsky, N. "The Formal Nature of Language." In Eric H. Lenneberg, *Biological Foundations of Language.* New York: John Wiley and Sons, 1967.

Chreist, F. M. *Foreign Accent.* Englewood Cliffs, N. J.: Prentice-Hall, Inc., 1964.

Corder, S. P. "Linguistics and Speech Therapy." *British Journal of Disorders of Speech* 1 (1966) : pp. 119–24.

Engel, R. C., Reid, W. R., and Rucker, D. P. *Language Development Experiences for Young Children.* Los Angeles: School of Education, University of California, 1966.

Farradane, J. "Relational Indexing and Classification in the Light of Recent Experimental Work in Psychology." *Information Storage and Retrieval* 1 (1963) : pp. 3–11.

Flanagan, J. L. *Speech Analysis, Synthesis and Perception.* New York: Academic Press, Inc., 1965.

Gibson, J. J. *The Senses Considered as Perceptual Systems.* Boston: Houghton-Mifflin, 1966.

Guilford, J. P. "Basic Conceptual Problems in the Psychology of Thinking." *Annals of the New York Academy of Science* 91 (1960) : pp. 6–21.

———"Three Faces of Intellect." *The American Psychologist* 14 (1959) : pp. 469–79.

Hempel, Carl G. *Fundamentals of Concept Formation in Empirical Science.* Chicago: University of Chicago Press, 1962.

Johnson, D. J., and Myklebust, H. R. *Learning Disabilities.* New York: Grune & Stratton, 1967.

Klausmeier, H. J., and Harris, C. W. *Analyses of Concept Learning.* New York: Academic Press, Inc., 1966.

Lado, R. "Pattern Practice—Completely Oral." *Language Learning* 16 (1966) : pp. 24–27.

Lenneberg, E. H. *Biological Foundations of Language.* New York: John Wiley & Sons, Inc., 1967.

Lieberman, P. *Intonation, Perception and Language.* Cambridge: M.I.T. Press, 1967.

Lin, S. C. *Pattern Practice in the Teaching of Standard English to Students with a Non-Standard English Dialect.* New York: Teachers College, Columbia University, 1965.

May, C. "A Language Stimulation Program for the Culturally Deprived Child." Unpublished problem. Albuquerque: University of New Mexico, 1968.

Marcel, G. *Metaphysical Journal.* Translated from the French by Bernard Wall. London: Rockliff, 1952.

Matson, F. W., and Montagu, A. *The Human Dialogue.* New York: Free Press, 1967.

McDonald, E. T. *Articulation Testing and Treatment: A Sensory-Motor Approach.* Pittsburgh: Stanwix House, Inc., 1964.

Mercer, E. H. *Cells: Their Structure and Function.* Garden City, N.Y.: Doubleday & Company, Inc., 1962.

Moses, E. R., Jr. *Phonetics: History and Interpretation.* Englewood Cliffs, N. J.: Prentice-Hall, Inc., 1964.

O'Malley, John B. *The Fellowship of Being.* The Hague: Martinus Nijoff, 1966.

Shannon, C. E., and Weaver, W. *The Mathematical Theory of Communication.* Urbana: University of Illinois Press, 1964.

Shen, Y. "Two English Modification Patterns for Chinese Students." *Language Learning* 16 (1966) : pp. 19–22.

Siegel, G. M. "Interpersonal Approaches to the Study of Communication Disorders." *Journal of Speech and Hearing Disorders* 32 (1967) : pp. 112–13.

Switzer, M. E. Foreword to *Research Needs in Speech Pathology and Audiology.* Monograph Supplement No. 5, *Journal of Speech and Hearing Disorders* (1959).

Tireman, L. S. *Teaching Spanish-Speaking Children.* Albuquerque: University of New Mexico Press, 1948.

Ward, J. A. *The Search for Form.* Chapel Hill: University of North Carolina Press, 1967.

Wood, K. S. "A Philosophy of Speech Correction." *Journal of Speech and Hearing Disorders* 12 (1947) : pp. 257–61.

Zintz, M. V. *Corrective Reading.* Dubuque, Iowa: Wm. C. Brown Company, 1966.

——— *Education Across Cultures.* Dubuque: Wm. C. Brown Company, 1963.

Chapter 3

Black, J. "The Quality of a Spoken Vowel." *Archives of Speech* 2 (1937) : pp. 7–27.

Daniloff, R. "A Cinefluorographic Study of Selected Aspects of Coarticulation of Speech Sounds." Ph.D. dissertation, University of Iowa, 1967.

Fairbanks, G., and Grubb, P. "A Psychophysical Investigation of Vowel Formants." *Journal of Speech and Hearing Research* 4 (1961) : pp. 203–19.

Halle, M. "On the Bases of Phonology." Chapter 9 in *The Structure of Language.* Edited by J. Fodor and J. Katz. Englewood Cliffs, N. J.: Prentice-Hall, Inc., 1964.

Kozhevnikov, V., and Chistovich, L. *Speech: Articulation and Perception.* Translated from *Rech: Artikulyatsiya i Vospriatiue,* Moscow-Leningrad, 1965. U.S. Department of Commerce, Joint Publications Research Service, 30, 543.

Lindblom, B. "Spectographic Study of Vowel Reduction." *Journal of the American Acoustical Society* 35 (1963) : pp. 1773–81.

Öhman, S. "Coarticulation in VCV Utterances: Spectographic Measurements." Ibid. 39 (1966) : pp. 151–68.

Peterson, G. "Information Bearing Elements of Speech." Ibid. 24 (1952) : pp. 629–37.

Stevens, K., and House, A. "Perturbations of Vowel Articulations by Consonanted Context: An Acoustical Study." *Journal of Speech and Hearing Research* 6 (1963) : pp. 111–28.

Chapter 4

Anisfield, M. "Evaluational Reactions to Accented-English Speech." *Research Bulletin on Intergroup Relations* 1 (1962).

Barbara, D. A., ed. *Psychological and Psychiatric Aspects of Speech and Hearing.* Springfield, Ill.: Charles C. Thomas, Publishers, 1960.

Bayley, Nancy. "Mental Growth During the First Three Years." In *Child Behavior and Development.* Edited by R. G. Barker, J. S. Kounin, and H. F. Wright. New York: McGraw-Hill, 1943, pp. 87–106.

Beckey, R. E. "A Study of Certain Factors Related to Retardation of Speech." *Journal of Speech and Hearing Disorders* 17 (1942) : pp. 273–79.

Bellugi, V. "The Development of Interrogative Structures in Children's Speech." In *The Development of Language Functions.* Edited by K. F. Riegel. Report No. 8, University of Michigan, Ann Arbor, 1965.

Berko, Jean. "The Child's Learning of English Morphology." *Word* 14 (1958) : pp. 150–77.

Bernstein, B. "Language and Social Class." *British Journal of Social and Clinical Psychology* 11 (1960) : pp. 271–76.

——"Linguistic Codes, Hesitation Phenomena and Intelligence." *Language and Speech* 5 (1962) : pp. 31–46. (a)

——"Social Class, Linguistic Codes and Grammatical Elements." Ibid. 5: pp. 221–40. (b)

——"Social Structure, Language and Learning." *Educational Research* 3 (1961) : pp. 163–76.

Bogoyavlenskiy, D. N. *Psikhologiya usvoyeniya orfografii.* Moscow: Akad. Pedag. Nauk RSFSR, 1957.

Bolinger, D. L. "Around the Edge of Language: Intonation." *Harvard Educational Review* 34 (1964) : pp. 282–96.

Bower, T. E. R. "Stimulus Variables Determining Space Perception in Infants." *Science* 34 (1965) : pp. 282–96.

Braine, M. D. S. "The Development of Speech and Language."

Unpublished manuscript. Walter Reed Army Hospital, Washington, D.C.

———"The Ontogeny of English Phrase Structure: The First Phase." *Language* 39 (1963) : pp. 1–13.

Brown, R. W. *Social Psychology*. New York: Free Press, 1965.

Brown, R., and Bellugi, Ursula. "Three Processes in the Child's Acquisition of Syntax." *Harvard Educational Review* 34 (1964) : pp. 133–51.

Chomsky, N. A. *Aspects of the Theory of Syntax*. Cambridge, Mass.: M.I.T. Press, 1965.

———Discussion of Miller and Ervin's paper. In *The Acquisition of Language*. Edited by Ursula Bellugi and R. Brown. *Monograph of Social Research in Child Development* 29 (1964) : pp. 35–39.

———"Topics in the Theory of Generative Grammar." *Current Trends in Linguistics*. Edited by Thomas Sebeok. The Hague, 1966, pp. 1–60.

Day, Ella J. "The Development of Language in Twins: I. A Comparison of Twins and Single Children." *Child Development* 3 (1932) : pp. 179–99.

Davis, I. P. "The Speech Aspects of Reading Readiness." *National Elementary Education* 17 (1938) : pp. 282–89.

Deutsch, M. "The Disadvantaged Child and the Learning Process." In *Education in Depressed Areas*. Edited by A. H. Passow. New York, 1963: Columbia University, Teachers College Bureau of Publications, pp. 163–79.

———"The Role of Social Class in Language Development and Cognition." *American Journal of Orthopsychiatry* 25 (1965) : pp. 78–88.

di Vesta, F. J. "A Simple Analysis of Changes with Age in Responses to a Restricted Word-Association Task: Grades 2 through 6." *Psychological Reports* 18 (1966) : pp. 65–66.

———"The Distribution of Modifiers Used by Children in a Word-Association Task." *Journal of Verbal Learning and Verbal Behavior* 3 (1964) : pp. 421–27.

di Vesta, F. J., and Dick, W. "The Test-Retest Reliability of Children's Ratings on the Semantic Differential." *Educational Psychology Measures* 26 (1966) : pp. 605–16.

Eisenberg, R., et al. "Auditory Behavior in the Human Neonate: A Preliminary Report." *Journal of Speech and Hearing Research* 7 (1964) : pp. 245–69.

Escalona, S. "The Use of Infant Tests for Predictive Purposes." In *Readings in Child Development.* Edited by W. E. Martin and C. B. Stendler. New York: Harcourt Brace, 1954, pp. 95–103.

Fairbanks, G. "Systematic Research in Experimental Phonetics." *Journal of Speech and Hearing Disorders* 19 (1954) .

Fant, G. *Acoustic Theory of Speech Production,* The Hague, 1960.

Frantz, R. "The Origin of Form Perception." *Scientific American* 204 (1961) : pp. 66–72.

Frazer, C., et al. "Control of Grammar in Imitation, Comprehension, and Production." *Journal of Verbal Learning and Verbal Behavior* 2 (1963) : pp. 121–35.

Glucksberg, S., Krauss, R. M., and Weisberg, R. "Referential Communication in Nursery School Children: Method and Some Preliminary Findings." *Journal of Experimental Child Psychology* 3 (1966) : pp. 333–42.

Glucksberg, S., and Krauss, R. M. "What Do People Say After They Have Learned to Talk? Studies of the Development of Referential Communication." *Merrill-Palmer Quarterly,* in press.

Gruber, J. "Topicalization in Child Language." *Foundations of Language* 3 (1967) : pp. 37–65.

Halle, M., and Stevens, K. N. "Speech Production: A Model and a Program for Research." In *The Structure of Language.* Edited by J. Katz and J. Fodor. Englewood Cliffs, N. J.: Prentice-Hall, Inc., 1964.

Hess, R. D., Shipman, V., and Jackson, D. "Early Experience and the Socialization of Cognitive Modes in Children." Paper read at American Association for Advancement of Science Symposium, Montreal, December, 1964.

Ibid., December, 1966.

Hollingshead, A. B., and Redlich, F. C. *Social Class and Mental Illness: A Community Study.* New York: John Wiley & Sons, Inc., 1958.

Hurst, Charles G. "A Preliminary Report on the 'Net Impact' of the United Planning Organization Target Area Programs" (with Roy Jones). *Technical Report,* The United Planning Organization, October, 1965.

———"Generating Spontaneous Speech in the Underprivileged Child." *The Journal of Negro Education,* Fall 1967.

———*Psychological Correlates in Dialectolalia.* The U. S. Office of Education, Department of Health, Education and Welfare. Cooperative Research Project 2610, November, 1965.

———"Psycho-Social Concomitants of Substandard Speech." *The Journal of Negro Education,* Yearbook, 1966.

———"Speech and Functional Intelligence." *Speech Monographs,* vol. 29 (June 1962).

Jakobson, R., and Halle, M. *Fundamentals of Language.* The Hague: Mouton, 1956.

———*Preliminaries to Speech Analysis.* Cambridge, Mass.: M.I.T. Press, 1952.

———*Kindersprache, Aphasie und Allgemeine Lautgesitze.* Uppsala, 1941.

John, Vera P. "The Intellectual Development of Slum Children: Some Preliminary Findings." *American Journal of Orthopsychiatry* 33 (1963) : pp. 813–22.

John, Vera P., and Goldstein, L. S. "The Social Context of Language Acquisition." *Merrill-Palmer Quarterly* 10 (1964) : pp. 249–63.

Kagan, J., and Lewis, M. "Studies of Attention in the Human Infant." *Merrill-Palmer Quarterly* 11 (1965) : pp. 95–127.

Katz, J. J., and Postal, P. *An Integrated Theory of Linguistic Descriptions.* Cambridge, Mass.: M.I.T. Press, 1964.

———"Recent Issues in Semantic Theory." *Foundations of Language 3* (1967) : pp. 124–94.

———*The Philosophy of Language.* New York, 1966. "The Structure of Semantic Theory." *Language* 39 (1963) : pp. 170–210.

Lane, H. "Development of Prosodic Features of Infants' Vocalizing." In *The Development of Language Functions.* Edited by K. F. Reigel. Report No. 8, University of Michigan, Ann Arbor, 1965.

Lees, R. B. Discussion of Brown and Fraser's, and Brown, Fraser, and Bellugi's papers. In *The Acquisition of Language.* Edited by Ursula Bellugi and R. Brown. *Monograph of Social Research in Child Development* 29 (1964) : pp. 92–97.

Lenneberg, E. H. *Biological Foundations of Language.* New York: John Wiley & Sons, Inc., 1967.

Leopold, W. F. *Speech Development of a Bilingual Child: A Linguist's Record.* Vol. 1. *Vocabulary Growth in the First Two Years.* Vol. 2. *Sound Learning in the First Two Years.* Vol. 3. *Grammar and General Problems in the First Two Years.* Vol. 4. *Diary from Age 2.* Evanston, Ill.: Northwestern University Press, 1939, 1947, 1949 (a) & (b).

Markel, N. "A Distinctive Feature Analysis of Pre-Linguistic Infant Vocalizations." In *The Development of Language Functions.* Edited by K. F. Riegel. Report No. 8, University of Michigan, Ann Arbor, 1965.

McCarthy, Dorothea. "The Language Development of the Pre-School Child." *Child Welfare Monograph,* 1930, no. 4.

McClure, H. S. "A Study of the Existing Relationships Between Articulatory Defects and Related Disabilities Including Reading." M.A. thesis, Ball State Teacher's College, 1952.

McNeill, D. "Developmental Psycholinguistics." In *The Genesis of Language: A Psycholinguistic Approach.* Edited by F. Smith and G. A. Miller. Cambridge, Mass.: M.I.T. Press, 1966.

———"The Creation of Language by Children." In *Psycholinguistic Papers.* Edited by J. Lyons and R. Wales. Edinburgh, Scotland: University of Edinburgh Press, 1966.

———"The Development of Language." In *Carmichael's Manual of Child Psychology*. Edited by P. A. Mussen. In press.

Messer, S. "Implicit Phonology in Children." *Journal of Verbal Learning and Verbal Behavior* 6 (1967) : pp. 609–13.

Miller, G. A., and Nicely, P. "An Analysis of Perceptual Confusions among English Consonants." *Journal of the Acoustical Society of America* 27 (1956) : pp. 338–52.

Miller, W., and Ervin, Susan. "The Development of Grammar in Child Language." In *The Acquisition of Language*. Edited by Ursula Bellugi and R. Brown. *Monograph of Social Research in Child Development* 29 (1964) : pp. 9–34.

Morehead, D. *Speech Recognition and Production in Young Children and Adults*. Ph.D. dissertation, Ohio State University, 1967.

Mowrer, O. H. *Learning and the Symbolic Processes*. New York: John Wiley & Sons, 1960.

Riegel, K. F., and Zivian, Irina, W. M. *A Study of Inter- and Intralingual Associations in English and German*. University of Michigan Language Development Program, Report No. 15, 1967.

———*The Michigan Restricted Association Norms*. University of Michigan Department of Psychology Report No. 3, 1965.

Ringwall, E. A., *et al.* "A Distinctive Feature Analysis of Pre-Linguistic Infant Vocalizations." In *The Development of Language Functions*. Edited by K. F. Riegel. Report No. 8, University of Michigan, Ann Arbor, 1967.

Sharf, D. J., *et al.* *A System for the Analysis of Speech Sound Development*. Report No. 14, University of Michigan, Ann Arbor, 1966.

Sheppard, W., and Lane, H. "Development of Prosodic Features in Infant Vocalizing." II in *Studies in Language Behavior*. Report No. 3, University of Michigan, Ann Arbor, 1966.

Shvachkin, N. "Raxvitiye fonematicheskogo vospriyatiya rechi v rannem vozraste." *Izv. Akad. Pedag. Navk RSFSR* 13 (1948) : pp. 101–32.

Slobin, D. I. Comments on "Developmental Psycholinguistics."

In *The Genesis of Language: A Psycholinguistic Approach.* Edited by F. Smith and G. A. Miller. Cambridge, Mass.: M.I.T. Press, 1966.

———"Grammatical Transformations in Childhood and Adulthood." Ph.D. dissertation, Harvard University, 1963.

———"The Acquisition of Russian as a Native Language." In *The Genesis of Language: A Psycholinguistic Approach.* Cambridge, Mass.: M.I.T. Press, 1966.

Stern, Clara, and Stern, W. *Die Kindersprache.* Leizig, 1907.

Stroud, R. "A Study of the Relations between Social Distances and Speech Differences of White and Negro High School Students of Dayton, Ohio." M.A. thesis, Bowling Green State University, 1956.

Templin, Mildred C. "Certain Language Skills in Children: Their Development and Interrelationships." *Child Welfare Monograph,* 1957, no. 26.

Wathen-Dunn, W., ed. *Models of Perception of Speech and Visual Form.* Cambridge, Mass.: M.I.T. Press, 1967.

Weinreich, U. "Explorations in Semantic Theory." In *Current Trends in Linguistics.* Edited by T. A. Sebeok. Vol. 3. The Hague: Mouton, 1966.

———"On the Semantic Structure of Language." In *Universals of Language.* Edited by J. H. Greenburg. Cambridge, Mass.: M.I.T. Press, 1962.

Weir, Ruth. *Language in the Crib.* The Hague: Mouton, 1962.

Whorf, B. J. "Linguistics as an Exact Science." In *Language, Thought, and Reality: Selected Writings of Benjamin Lee Whorf.* Edited by J. B. Carroll. Cambridge, Mass.: M.I.T. Press, 1956.

Chapter 5

Berko, J. "The Child's Learning of English Morphology." *Word* 14 (1953) : pp. 150–77.

Brown, R. W. "Linguistic Determinism and the Part of Speech."

Journal of Abnormal and Social Psychology 55 (1957) : pp. 1–5.

Cazden, C. "On Individual Differences in Language Differences in Language Competence and Performance." *Journal of Special Education* 1 (1968) : p. 2.

Chomsky, N. *Syntactic Structures*. Gravehage, the Netherlands, 1957.

———*Aspects of the Theory of Syntax*. Cambridge, Mass.: M.I.T. Press, 1965.

Cooper, R. L. "The Ability of Deaf and Hearing Children to Apply Morphological Rules." *Journal of Speech and Hearing Research* 10 (1967) : pp. 77–85.

Ervin, S. M. "Imitation and Structural Change in Children's Language. In *New Directions in the Study of Language*. Edited by E. H. Lenneberg. Cambridge, Mass.: M.I.T. Press, 1964.

Fodor, J. and Garrett. "Thoughts on Competence and Performance." *Psycholinguistic Papers. Proceedings, 1966 Edinburgh Conference,* Edinburgh University Press, 1966.

Glaze, J. A. "The Association Value of Nonsense Syllables." *Journal of Genetic Psychology* 35 (1929) : pp. 255–67.

Gussow, J. "Language Development in Disadvantaged Children." *IRCD Bulletin* 1 (1965) : p. 5.

Hurst, C. G., and Jones, W. L. "Psychosocial Concomitants of Substandard Speech." *Journal of Negro Education,* Fall 1966.

Lee, L. L. "Developmental Sentence Types: A Method for Comparing Normal and Deviant Syntactic Development." *Journal of Speech and Hearing Disorders* 31 (1933) : pp. 311–30.

Mednick, S. A. *Learning*. Englewood Cliffs, N. J.: Prentice-Hall, Inc., 1964.

McNeill, D. "Developmental Psycholinguistics," in *The Genesis of Language*. Edited by F. Smith and G. A. Miller. Cambridge, Mass.: M.I.T. Press, 1966.

Menyuk, P. "Syntactic Structures in the Language of Children." *Child Development* 34 (1963a) : pp. 407–22.

————"A Preliminary Evaluation of Grammatical Capacity in Children." *Journal of Verbal Learning and Verbal Behavior* 2 (1963b) : pp. 429–39.

————"Syntactic Rules Used by Children from Preschool Through First Grade." *Child Development* 35 (1964a) : pp. 533–43.

————"Alternation of Rules in Children's Grammar." *Journal of Verbal Learning and Verbal Behavior* 3 (1964) b) : pp. 480–88.

————"Comparison of Grammar of Children with Functionally Deviant and Normal Speech." *Journal of Speech and Hearing Research* 7 (1964c) : pp. 109–21.

Noble, C. E. "Verbal Learning and Individual Differences." *Verbal Learning and Verbal Behavior.* Edited by C. Cofer and B. Musgrave. New York, McGraw-Hill, 1961.

Quay, H. C. *The Facets of Educational Exceptionality: A Conceptual Framework for Assessment, Grouping and Instruction.* Champaign, Ill., 1968.

Shriner, T. H., and Miner, L. "Morphological Structures in the Language of Disadvantaged and Advantaged Children." *Journal of Speech and Hearing Research* 11, in press, 1968.

Wales, R. J., and Marshal, J. C. "The Organization of Linguistic Performance." *Psycholinguistic Papers. Proceedings, 1966 Edinburgh Conference,* Edinburgh University Press, 1966.

Williams, F., and Naremore, R. C. *Language and Poverty: An Annotated Bibliography.* Institute for Research on Poverty. Madison, Wis., 1967.

Zeaman, D., and House, B. J. "The Relation of IQ and Learning." In *Learning and Individual Differences.* Edited by R. M. Gagne. Columbus, Ohio, 1966.

Chapter 6

Carter, E. T., and Buck, M. "Prognostic Testing for Functional Articulation Disorders Among Children in the First Grade."

Journal of Speech and Hearing Disorders 26 (1953) : pp. 124–33.

Keppel, G. "Retroactive Inhibition of Serial Lists as a Function of the Presence of Positional Cues." *Journal of Verbal Learning and Verbal Behavior* 3 (1964) : pp. 511–17.

Postman, L. "The Temporal Course of Proactive Inhibition for Serial Lists." *Journal of Experimental Psychology* 63 (1962) : pp. 361–69.

Rice, D. B., and Milisen, R. "The Influence of Increased Stimulation upon the Production of Unfamiliar Sounds as a Function of Time." *Journal of Speech and Hearing Disorders* [Monograph Supplement] 4 (1954) : pp. 79–86.

Scott, D. A., and Milisen, R. "The Effectiveness of Combined Visual-Auditory Stimulation in Improving Articulation." *Ibid.* 4: pp. 51–56.

Underwood, B. J. "Interference and Forgetting." *Psychological Review,* 64 (1957) : pp. 49–60.

Underwood, B. J., and Ekstrand, B. R. "Word Frequency and Accumulative Proactive Inhibition." *Journal of Experimental Psychology* 74 (1967) : pp. 193–98.

Underwood, B. J., and Postman, L. "Extraexperimental Sources of Interference in Forgetting." *Psychological Review* 67 (1960) : pp. 73–95.

Underwood, B. J., and Schulz, R. W. *Meaningfulness and Verbal Learning.* Philadelphia: Lippincott, 1960.

Winitz, H. *Articulatory Acquisition and Behavior.* New York: Appleton-Century-Crofts, 1969.

Winitz, H., and Bellerose, B. "Phoneme-Cluster Learning as a Function of Instructional Method and Age." *Journal of Verbal Learning and Verbal Behavior* 4 (1965) : pp. 98–102.

———"Relation between Sound Discrimination and Sound Learning." *Journal of Communication Disorders,* 1 (1967) : pp. 215–35.

———"Proactive Interference and Articulatory Retention." Unpublished study, 1968.

Winitz, H., and Lawrence, M. "Children's Articulation and Sound Learning Ability." *Journal of Speech and Hearing Research* 4 (1961) : pp. 259–68.

Winitz, H., and Preisler, L. "Discrimination Pretaining and Sound Learning." *Perceptual and Motor Skills* 20 (1965) : pp. 905–16.

———"Effect of Distinctive Feature Pretraining in Phoneme Discrimination Learning." *Journal of Speech and Hearing Research* 10 (1967) : pp. 315–30.

Chapter 7

Denes, P. B. "On the Statistics of Spoken English." *Journal of the Acoustical Society of America* 35 (1963) : pp. 892–904.

Halle, M. "On the Role of Simplicity in Linguistic Descriptions." American Mathematical Society, Proceedings of Symposia in Applied Mathematics, Structure of Language and its Mathematical Aspects, 12 (1961) : pp. 89–94.

Irwin, O. C. "Infant Speech: Consonant Sounds According to Manner of Articulation." *Journal of Speech Disorders* 12 (1947) : pp. 397–401.

Jakobson, R. *Selected Writings* The Netherlands: Mouton, 1960: I, pp. 317–402, 491–503, 538–46.

Jakobson, R., Fant, C. G., and Halle, M. *Preliminaries to Speech Analysis.* Cambridge, Mass.: M.I.T. Press, 1963.

Menyuk, P. "Syntactic Rules Used by Children from Pre-School Through First Grade." *Journal of Child Development* 35 (1964a) : pp. 533–46.

———"Comparison of Grammar of Children with Normal and Deviant Speech." *Journal of Speech and Hearing Research* 7 (1964b) : pp. 109–21.

Nakzima, S., Okamoto, N., Murai, J., Tanaka, M., Okuno, S., Maeda, T., and Shimizu, M. "The Phoneme Systemization and the Verbalization Process of Voices in Childhood." *Shinrigan-Hyoron* 6 (1962) : pp. 1–48.

Powers, M. H. "Functional Disorders of Articulation-Symptomatology and Etiology." In *Handbook of Speech Pathology.* Edited by L. E. Travis. New York: Appleton-Century-Crofts, 1957.

Templin, M. C., and Darley, F. L. *The Templin-Darley Tests of Articulation.* Iowa City: State University of Iowa, Bureau of Educational Research and Service, Extension Division, 1960.

Wicklegren, W. A. "Distinctive Features and Errors in Short-Term Memory for English Consonants." *Journal of the Acoustical Society of America* 39 (1966) : pp. 388–98.

BIBLIOGRAPHY

ABE, I. INTONATION PATTERNS OF ENGLISH AND JAPANESE WORD, 11, 386–398, 1955.

ALBRIGHT, J. S. AND ALBRIGHT, R. W. THE ROLE OF LINGUISTICS IN SPEECH AND HEARING THERAPY, LANGUAGE LEARNING, IX, 1959, 51–55.

ALBRIGHT, R. AND ALBRIGHT, J. APPLICATION OF DESCRIPTIVE LINGUISTICS TO CHILD LANGUAGE, JOURNAL OF SPEECH AND HEARING RESEARCH, 1965, 1, 257–261.

ALGER, D. MATERIALS DUPLICATED FOR USE IN THE WORKSHOP ON SECOND-LANGUAGE TEACHING, JUNE 11–22, 1962, DIVISION OF INDIAN EDUCATION, N. M. STATE DEPARTMENT OF EDUCATION.

ALLEN, H. B. MINOR DIALECT AREAS OF THE UPPER MIDWEST, PUBLICATION OF THE AMERICAN DIALECT SOCIETY, NO. 30 (1958), PP. 3–16.

ALLEN, H. B. CANADIAN-AMERICAN SPEECH DIFFERENCES ALONG THE MIDDLE BORDER, JOURNAL OF THE CANADIAN LINGUISTIC ASSOCIATION, V, I (SPRING, 1959), 17–24.

ALLISON, V. C. ON THE OZARK PRONUNCIATION OF IT, AMERICAN SPEECH IV, 1929, PP. 205–206.

ALLPORT, F. H. SOCIAL PSYCHOLOGY, BOSTON HOUGHTON MIFFLIN COMPANY, 1924.

ANASTASIA, A. AND D'ANGELO, R. A COMPARISON OF NEGRO AND WHITE PRESCHOOL CHILDREN IN LANGUAGE DEVELOPMENT AND GOODENOUGH DRAW-A-MAN IQ, JOURNAL OF GENETIC PSYCHOLOGY, 1952, 81, 147–165.

ANASTASI, A. AND DEJESUS, C. LANGUAGE DEVELOPMENT AND NONVERBAL IQ OF PUERTO RICAN PRESCHOOL CHILDREN IN NEW YORK CITY, THE JOURNAL OF ABNORMAL AND SOCIAL PSYCHOLOGY, 1953, 48, 357–366.

ANDERSON, V. A. TRAINING OF THE SPEAKING VOICE, NEW YORK OXFORD UNIVERSITY PRESS, 1961.

ANISFELD, M. EVALUATIONAL REAC-
TIONS TO ACCENTED-ENGLISH SPEECH,
RESEARCH BULLETIN ON INTERGROUP
RELATIONS, 1, 3 (1962).

ANSHEN, R. W., ED. LANGUAGE, AN
ENQUIRY INTO ITS MEANING AND
FUNCTION, NEW YORK HARPER AND
ROW, PUBLISHERS, 1957.

ANSHER, R. N. LANGUAGE, AN IDEA
LANGUAGE, AN ENQUIRY INTO ITS
MEANING AND FUNCTION, NEW YORK
HARPER AND ROW, PUBLISHERS. INC.,
1957.

ARMSTRONG, L. E. AND WARD,
I. C. HANDBOOK OF ENGLISH INTONA-
TION, B. G. TEUBNER, LEIPZIG AND
BERLIN, 1926.

ATWOOD, E. B. A PRELIMINARY RE-
PORT ON TEXAS WORD GEOGRAPHY,
ORBIS, II (JAN., 1953), 61–66.

ATWOOD, E. B. A SURVEY OF VERB
FORMS IN THE EASTERN UNITED
STATES, ANN ARBOR UNIVERSITY OF
MICHIGAN PRESS, 1953.

ATWOOD, E. B. THE METHODS OF
AMERICAN DIALECTOLOGY, ZEITSCH-
RIFT FUR MUNDARTFORSCHUNG, XXX
(OCT., 1963), 1–30.

ATWOOD, E. B. THE REGIONAL VO-
CABULARY OF TEXAS, AUSTIN UNIVER-
SITY OF TEXAS PRESS, 1962.

ATWOOD, E. B. A SURVEY OF VERB
FORMS IN THE EASTERN UNITED
STATES, ANN ARBOR, MICH., 1953.

AUSUBEL, D. P. HOW REVERSIBLE ARE
THE COGNITIVE AND MOTIVATIONAL
EFFECTS OF CULTURAL DEPRIVATION,
IMPLICATIONS FOR TEACHING THE
CULTURALLY DEPRIVED CHILD, URBAN
EDUCATION, 1964, 1, 16–38.

AVIS, WALTER S. THE MID-BACK
VOWELS IN THE ENGLISH OF THE
EASTERN UNITED STATES, A DETAILED
INVESTIGATION OF REGIONAL AND SO-
CIAL DIFFERENCES IN PHONIC CHAR-
ACTERISTICS AND PHONEMIC ORGANI-
ZATION, DOCTORAL DISSERTATION,
UNIVERSITY OF MICHIGAN, 1956
MICROFILM.

AVIS, W. S. SPEECH DIFFERENCES
ABOVE THE ONTARIO-UNITED STATES
BORDER, JOURNAL OF THE CANADIAN
LINGUISTIC ASSOCIATION, I, I (OCT.,
1954), 13–17, I, I (REGULAR SERIES,
MARCH, 1956), 14–19 II, II (OCT.,
1956), 41–59.

AXLEY, L. WEST VIRGINIA DIALECT,
AMERICAN SPEECH III, 1928, P. 456.

BABINGTON, M. AND ATWOOD,
E. B. LEXICAL USAGE IN SOUTHERN
LOUISIANA, PUBLICATION OF THE
AMERICAN DIALECT SOCIETY, NO. 36
(NOV., 1961), PP. 1–24.

BAILEY, B. L. A PROPOSAL FOR THE
STUDY OF THE GRAMMAR OF NEGRO
ENGLISH IN NEW YORK CITY, PROJECT
LITERACY REPORTS, NO. 2, ITHACA,
NEW YORK, CORNELL UNIV., 1964, 19–
22.

BAILEY, E. B. THE NEGRO IN EAST
TENNESSEE, THESIS, NEW YORK UNI-
VERSITY, 1947.

BANDURA, A. AND McDONALD,
F. J. THE INFLUENCE OF SOCIAL RE-
INFORCEMENT AND THE BEHAVIOR OF
MODELS IN SHAPING CHILDREN'S
MORAL JUDGMENTS, JOURNAL OF AB-
NORMAL SOCIAL PSYCHOLOGY, 1963,
67, 274–281.

BARATZ, J. AND POVICH, E. GRAM-
MATICAL CONSTRUCTIONS AND THE
LANGUAGE OF THE PRESCHOOL NEGRO
CHILD, PAPER PRESENTED AT 1967
ASHA CONVENTION.

BARBER, C. LINGUISTIC CHANGE IN PRESENT-DAY ENGLISH, UNIVERSITY OF ALABAMA PRESS, UNIVERSITY, ALA., 1965.

BARKER, J. L. CORRECTING THE MECHANISM CAUSING MOST FOREIGN BROGUE, JOURNAL OF SPEECH DISORDERS, I (1936), NO. 1, 3–12.

BARTLETT, J. R. DICTIONARY OF AMERICANISM, A GLOSSARY OF WORDS AND PHRASES USUALLY REGARDED AS PECULIAR TO THE UNITED STATES, 2ND ED. BOSTON, 1859.

BATES, M. MAN IN NATURE, ENGLEWOOD CLIFFS, N. J., PRENTICE-HALL, INC., 1961.

BAYNHAM, D. THE GREAT CITIES PROJECTS, NATIONAL EDUCATIONAL ASSOCIATION JOURNAL, 1963, 52, 17–20.

BEALS, R. L. AND HOIJER, H. AN INTRODUCTION TO ANTHROPOLOGY, NEW YORK, THE MACMILLAN COMPANY, 1959.

BEEBE, H. H. AUDITORY MEMORY SPAN FOR MEANINGLESS SYLLABLES, JOURNAL OF SPEECH DISORDERS, IX (1944), 273–75.

BELLAK, L. AND BELLAK, S. CHILDREN'S APPERCEPTION TEST (C. A. T.) LARCHMONT, N. Y., C. P. S., INC., 1964.

BERKO, J. THE CHILD'S LEARNING OF ENGLISH MORPHOLOGY, WORD, 1958, 14, 150–177.

BERLO, D. K. THE PROCESS OF COMMUNICATION, NEW YORK, HOLT, RINEHART AND WINSTON, INC., 1960.

BERNSTEIN, B. FAMILY ROLE SYSTEMS, COMMUNICATION, AND SOCIALIZATION, UNPUBLISHED PAPER PREPARED FOR THE CONFERENCE ON DEVELOPMENT OF CROSS-NATIONAL RESEARCH ON THE EDUCATION OF CHILDREN AND ADOLESCENTS, UNIVERSITY OF CHICAGO, (FEBRUARY 20–28, 1964).

BERNSTEIN, B. SOCIAL CLASS AND LINGUISTIC DEVELOPMENT, A THEORY OF SOCIAL LEARNING, HALSEY, A. H., FLOUD, JEAN, AND ANDERSON, C. A. (EDS), EDUCATION, ECONOMY AND SOCIETY. ILLINOIS FREE PRESS OF GLENCOE, (1961).

BERNSTEIN, B. A SOCIO-LINGUISTIC APPROACH TO SOCIAL LEARNING, JULIUS GOULD, ED., PENGUIN SURVEY OF THE SOCIAL SCIENCES, 1965. BALTIMORE, MARYLAND, PENGUIN BOOKS, 1965.

BERNSTEIN, B. LINGUISTIC CODES, HESITATION PHENOMENA AND INTELLIGENCE, LANGUAGE AND SPEECH, 1962, 5, 31–46.

BERNSTEIN, B. SOCIAL CLASS, LINGUISTIC CODES AND GRAMMATICAL ELEMENTS, LANGUAGE AND SPEECH, 1962, 5, 221–240.

BERNSTEIN, B. SOME SOCIOLOGICAL DETERMINANTS OF PERCEPTION, BRITISH JOURNAL OF SOCIOLOGY, 1958, 9, 159–174.

BERNSTEIN, B. A PUBLIC LANGUAGE, SOME SOCIOLOGICAL IMPLICATION OF A LINGUISTIC FORM, BRITISH JOURNAL OF SOCIOLOGY, 1959, 10, 311–326.

BERNSTEIN, B. LANGUAGE AND SOCIAL CLASS (RESEARCH NOTE) BRITISH JOURNAL OF SOCIOLOGY, 1960, 11, 271–276.

BERNSTEIN, B. ASPECTS OF LANGUAGE AND LEARNING IN THE GENESIS OF THE SOCIAL PROCESS, JOURNAL OF CHILD PSYCHOLOGY AND PSYCHIATRY, 1961, 1, 313–324.

BERNSTEIN, B. ELABORATED AND RESTRICTED CODES, THEIR SOCIAL ORIGINS AND SOME CONSEQUENCES, GUMPERZ, J. AND HYMES, D. EDS. THE ETHNOGRAPHY OF COMMUNICATION, AMERICAN ANTHROPOLOGIST, SPECIAL PUBLICATION, 1964, 66, NO. 6, PART 2, 55–69.

BERNSTEIN, B. A PUBLIC LANGUAGE, SOME SOCIOLOGICAL IMPLICATIONS OF A LINGUISTIC FORM, BRIT. J. SOCIOLOGY, 1959, 10, 311–336.

BERRY, L. V. SOUTHERN MOUNTAIN DIALECT, AMERICAN SPEECH XV, 1940, PP. 45–54.

BERRY, M. AND EISENSON, J. SPEECH DISORDERS, PRINCIPLES OF THERAPY, NEW YORK, APPLETON-CENTURY-CROFTS, 1956.

BIRDWHISTELL, R. L. INTRODUCTION TO KINESICS, WASHINGTON, D. C., DEPARTMENT OF STATE FOREIGN SERVICE INSTITUTE, 1952.

BLACK, J. W., SINGH, S., TOSI, O., TAKEFUTA, Y., AND JANCOSEK, E. G. RELATIONSHIP BETWEEN SPEECH AND AURAL COMPREHENSION IN THE ENGLISH OF FOREIGN STUDENTS, JOURNAL OF SPEECH AND HEARING RESEARCH, 8, 43–48 (1965).

BLACK, J. W. AND MOORE, W. E. SPEECH, CODE, MEANING AND COMMUNICATION, NEW YORK, MCGRAW-HILL BOOK COMPANY, 1955.

BLOOMFIELD, L. LITERATE AND ILLITERATE SPEECH, AMERICAN SPEECH, 1927, 2, 432–439.

BLOOMFIELD, L. LANGUAGE, NEW YORK, HOLT, RINEHART AND WINSTON, INC., 1933.

BLOOM, B. S., DAVIS, A., AND HESS, R. COMPENSATORY EDUCATION FOR CULTURAL DEPRIVATION, NEW YORK, HOLT, RINEHART AND WINSTON, 1965.

BLACK, J., HURST, C., AND SINGH, S. SELF-ADMINISTERED PROCEDURES IN CHANGING PRONUNCIATION DIALECT, JOURNAL SPEECH AND HEARING RESEARCH, (IN PRESS).

BOAS, F. GENERAL ANTHROPOLOGY, WAR DEPARTMENT EDUCATIONAL MANUAL, BOSTON, D. C. HEATH AND COMPANY, 1938.

BOLINGER, D. L. A THEORY OF PITCH ACCENT IN ENGLISH, WORD, 14, 109–149, 1958.

BOLINGER, D. INTONATION LEVELS VERSUS CONFIGURATION, WORD, VII, DECEMBER, 1951.

BOLINGER, D. STRESS AND INFORMATION, AMERICAN SPEECH, XXXIII, FEBRUARY, 1958.

BORRECA, F. A., BURGER, R., GOLDSTEIN, I., AND SIMCHES, R. A. FUNCTIONAL CORE VOCABULARY FOR SLOW LEARNERS, AMERICAN JOURNAL OF MENTAL DEFICIENCY, 1953, 58, 273–300.

BOSSARD, J. H. S. FAMILY MODES OF EXPRESSION, CHAPTER 9 IN BOSSARD, THE SOCIOLOGY OF CHILD DEVELOPMENT, NEW YORK, HARPER AND BROTHERS, 1948.

BOWER, W. A. INTERNATIONAL MANUAL OF LINGUISTS AND TRANSLATORS, FIRST SUPPLEMENT, NEW YORK, THE SCARECROW PRESS, INC., 1961.

BRAIDWOOD, R. J. PREHISTORIC MAN, 5TH ED., CHICAGO, CHICAGO NATURAL HISTORY MUSEUM, 1961.

BRAIN, L. SPEECH DISORDERS, APHASIA, APRAXIA AND AGNOSIA, WASHING-

TON, D. C., BUTTERWORTH AND CO., 1961.

BRAY, R. A. DISAPPEARING DIALECT, ANTIOCH REVIEW, X, 1950, PP. 279–288.

BRAZZIEL, W. F. CORRELATES OF SOUTHERN NEGRO PERSONALITY, JOURNAL OF SOCIAL ISSUES, 20, 46–53 (1964).

BRAZZIEL, W. R. AND TERRELL, M. AN EXPERIMENT IN THE DEVELOP-MENT OF READINESS IN A CULTURAL-LY DISADVANTAGED GROUP OF FIRST-GRADE CHILDREN, JOURNAL OF NEGRO EDUCATION, 1962, 31, 4–7.

BRENGELMAN, F. H. THE NATIVE AMERICAN ENGLISH SPOKEN IN THE PUGET SOUND AREA, DOCTORAL DIS-SERTATION, UNIVERSITY OF WASHING-TON, 1957.

BRITTAIN, C. V. PRESCHOOL PRO-GRAMS FOR CULTURALLY DEPRIVED CHILDREN, CHILDREN, 1966, 13, 130–134.

BRONG, C. C. AN EVALUATION OF EAR TRAINING AS A PEDAGOGICAL TECH-NIQUE IN IMPROVING SOUND DISCRIM-INATION, UNPUBLISHED DOCTORAL DISSERTATION, NORTHWESTERN UNI-VERSITY, 1948.

BRONSTEIN, A. J. THE PRONUNCIA-TION OF AMERICAN ENGLISH, NEW YORK, APPLETON-CENTURY-CROFTS, 1960.

BROOKS, C. JR. THE RELATION OF THE ALABAMA-GEORGIA DIALECT TO THE PROVINCIAL DIALECTS OF GREAT BRITIAN, BATON ROUGE, LOUISIANA STATE UNIVERSITY PRESS, 1935.

BROOKS, N. LANGUAGE AND LAN-GUAGE LEARNING, NEW YORK, HAR-COURT, BRACE AND WORLD, INC., 1960.

BROOK, G. L. ENGLISH DIALECTS, LONDON, 1964.

BROPHY, J., SHIPMAN, V. C., AND HESS, R. D. EFFECTS OF SOCIAL CLASS AND LEVEL OF ASPIRATION ON PERFORMANCE IN A STRUCTURED MOTHER-CHILD INTERACTION, UNPUB-LISHED PAPER PRESENTED AT BIEN-NIAL MEETING OF THE SOCIETY FOR RESEARCH IN CHILD DEVELOPMENT, MINNEAPOLIS, (MARCH 24, 1965).

BROSNAHAN, L. F. THE SOUNDS OF LANGUAGE, AN INQUIRY INTO THE ROLE OF GENETIC FACTORS IN THE DEVELOPMENT OF SOUND SYSTEMS, CAMBRIDGE, W. HEFFER AND SONS, LTD., 1961.

BROWN, J. S. THE SOCIAL ORGANIZA-TION OF AN ISOLATED KENTUCKY MOUNTAIN NEIGHBORHOOD, PH.D. DISSERTATION, HARVARD UNIVERSITY, 1950.

BROWN, J. S. CONJUGAL FAMILY AND THE EXTENDED FAMILY GROUP, AMERICAN SOCIOLOGICAL REVIEW, XVII, 1952, PP. 297–306.

BROWN, J. S. THE FARM FAMILY IN A KENTUCKY MOUNTAIN NEIGHBOR-HOOD, KENTUCKY AGRICULTURAL EX-PERIMENT STATION BULLETIN 587, 1952.

BROWN, J. S. THE FAMILY GROUP IN A KENTUCKY MOUNTAIN FARMING COMMUNITY, KENTUCKY AGRICUL-TURAL EXPERIMENT STATION BULLE-TIN 588, 1958.

BROWN, R. AND BELLUGI, U. THREE PROCESSES IN THE CHILD'S AC-QUISITION OF SYNTAX, HARVARD EDU-CATIONAL REVIEW, 1964, 34, 133–151.

BROWN, R. W. AND FORD, M. AD-

DRESS IN AMERICAN ENGLISH, JOUR-
NAL OF ABNORMAL AND SOCIAL PSY-
CHOLOGY, 1961, 62, 375–385.

BROWN, R. WORDS AND THINGS,
GLENCOE, ILL., THE FREE PRESS, 1958.

BRYANT, M. M. CURRENT AMERICAN
USAGE, NEW YORK, 1962.

BUHLER, K. THE MENTAL DEVELOP-
MENT OF THE CHILD, LONDON, ROUT-
LEDGE AND KEGAN PAUL, LTD., 1930.

BURSSENS, A. NOTES ON AFRICAN
TONE LANGUAGES, MANUAL OF PHO-
NETICS, L. KAISER, ED., AMSTERDAM,
NORTH-HOLLAND PUBLISHING COM-
PANY, 1947.

BUTLER, H. E. THE INSTITUTIO
ORATORIA OF QUINTILLIAN, 4 VOLS.,
LONDON, CAMBRIDGE UNIVERSITY
PRESS, WILLIAM HEINEMAN, LTD.,
1953.

CALDWELL, B. AND RICHMOND,
J. B. PROGRAMMED DAY CARE FOR
THE VERY YOUNG CHILD, A PRELIMI-
NARY REPORT, JOURNAL OF MAR-
RIAGE AND THE FAMILY, 1964, 26,
481–488.

CAMPBELL, J. C. THE SOUTHERN
HIGHLANDER AND HIS HOMELAND,
NEW YORK, THE RUSSELL SAGE FOUN-
DATION, 1927.

CAMPBELL, G. A. TELEPHONIC IN-
TELLIGIBILITY, LONDON, EDINBURGH,
DUBLIN, PHILOSOPHICAL MAGAZINE
AND JOURNAL OF SCIENCE, XIX,
JANUARY, 1910.

CANSLER, C. W. THREE GENERA-
TIONS, THE STORY OF A COLORED
FAMILY OF EASTERN TENNESSEE,
KINGSPORT, KINGSPORT PRESS, 1939.

CAPELL, A. STUDIES IN SOCIO-LIN-
GUISTICS, THE HAGUE, MOUTON AND
CO., 1966.

CAPLAN, S. AND RUBLE, R. A STUDY
OF CULTURALLY IMPOSED FACTORS ON
SCHOOL ACHIEVEMENT IN A METRO-
POLITAN AREA, THE JOURNAL OF ED-
UCATIONAL RESEARCH, 1964, 58, 16–
21.

CARHART, R. AUDITORY TRAINING
IN HEARING AND DEAFNESS, REV. ED.,
HALLOWELL DAVIS, ED., NEW YORK,
HOLT, RINEHART AND WINSTON, INC.,
1960, PP. 368–86.

CARPENTER, C. VARIATION IN THE
SOUTHERN   MOUNTAIN   DIALECT,
AMERICAN SPEECH, VIII, 1933, PP. 22–
25.

CARRELL, J. A. A COMPARATIVE
STUDY OF SPEECH DEFECTIVE CHIL-
DREN, UNPUBLISHED DOCTORAL DIS-
SERTATION, NORTHWESTERN UNIVER-
SITY, 1946.

CARRELL, J. AND TIFFANY, W.
PHONETICS THEORY AND APPLICATION
TO SPEECH IMPROVEMENT, NEW
YORK, MCGRAW-HILL BOOK COM-
PANY, 1960.

CARROLL, J. B. THE STUDY OF LAN-
GUAGES, A SURVEY OF LINGUISTICS
AND RELATED DISCIPLINES IN AMER-
ICA, CAMBRIDGE, MASS., HARVARD
UNIVERSITY PRESS, 1953.

CARROW, M. LINGUISTIC FUNCTION-
ING OF BILINGUAL AND MONOLIN-
GUAL CHILDREN, JOURNAL OF SPEECH
AND HEARING DISORDERS, XXII, 1957.

CARSON, A. S. AND RABIN, A. I.
VERBAL COMPREHENSION AND COM-
MUNICATION IN NEGRO AND WHITE
CHILDREN, THE JOURNAL OF EDUCA-
TIONAL PSYCHOLOGY, 1960, 51, 47–
51.

CARTRIGHT, R. W. ON MACHINES

AND MEN, THE SOUTHERN SPEECH JOURNAL, XXVIII, SUMMER 1963.

CASSIDY, F. G. SOME NEW ENGLAND WORDS IN WISCONSIN, LANGUAGE, XVII (OCT.–DEC., 1941), 324–339.

CAVE, R. H. THE IDENTIFICATION AND MEASUREMENT OF ENVIRONMENTAL PROCESS VARIABLES THAT ARE RELATED TO EDUCATIONAL ACHIEVEMENT, UNPUBLISHED DOCTORAL DISSERTATION, UNIVERSITY OF CHICAGO, 1963.

CAZDEN, C. B. SUBCULTURAL DIFFERENCES IN CHILD LANGUAGE, AN INTERDISCIPLINARY REVIEW, MERRILL PALMER QUARTERLY, 1966, 12, 185–219.

CHAIKLIN, J. B. NATIVE AMERICAN LISTENERS' ADAPTATION IN UNDERSTANDING SPEAKERS WITH FOREIGN DIALECT, JOURNAL OF SPEECH AND HEARING DISORDERS, XX, JUNE, 1955.

CHAPMAN, M. AMERICAN SPEECH AS PRACTISED IN THE SOUTHERN HIGHLANDS, CENTURY, MARCH, 1929.

CHERRY, C. ON HUMAN COMMUNICATION, CAMBRIDGE, MASS., THE TECHNOLOGY PRESS OF THE MASS. INSTITUTE OF TECH., NEW YORK, JOHN WILEY AND SONS, INC., BOTH 1959.

CHOMSKY, N. AND MILLER, G. A. INTRODUCTION TO THE FORMAL ANALYSIS OF NATURAL LANGUAGES, LUCE, R. D., BUSH, R. B. AND GALANTER, E., EDS., HANDBOOK OF MATHEMATICAL PSYCHOLOGY, VOL. 1, NEW YORK, WILEY, 1963, 269–321.

CHOMSKY, N. AND HALLE, M. THE SOUND PATTERN OF ENGLISH, HARPER AND ROW, NEW YORK, 1966.

CHOMSKY, N., HALLE, M., AND LUKOFF, F. ON ACCENT AND JUNCTURE IN ENGLISH, FOR ROMAN JAKOBSON, M. HALLE, H. LUNT, AND H. MACLEAN, EDS., MOUTON, THE NETHERLANDS, HAGUE, 1956.

CHOMSKY, N. SYNTACTIC STRUCTURES, THE HAGUE, MOUTON AND COMPANY, 1957.

CHREIST, FRED M. FOREIGN ACCENT, PRENTICE-HALL, INC., ENGLEWOOD CLIFFS, NEW JERSEY, 1964.

CLARK, A. AND RICHARDS, C. AUDITORY DISCRIMINATION AMONG ECONOMICALLY DISADVANTAGED AND NONDISADVANTAGED PRESCHOOL CHILDREN, EXCEPTIONAL CHILDREN, 1966, 33, 259–262.

CLARK, W. P. THE INDIAN SIGN LANGUAGE, PHILADELPHIA, L. R. HAMMERSLEY AND COMPANY, 1885.

CLOUGH, W. O. SOME WYOMING SPEECH PATTERNS, AMERICAN SPEECH, XXIX (FEB., 1954), 28–35.

COFFEE, N. M. THE PHONEMIC STRUCTURE OF UNSTRESSED VOWELS IN ENGLISH, AMERICAN SPEECH, XXVI, FEBRUARY, 1951, NO. 1.

COHEN, A. B. UPWARD COMMUNICATION IN EXPERIMENTALLY CREATED HIERARCHIES, HUMAN RELATIONS, 1958, 11, 41–53.

COHN, W. ON THE LANGUAGE OF LOWER-CLASS CHILDREN, THE SCHOOL REVIEW, 1959, 67, 435–440.

COLEMAN, W. MOUNTAIN DIALECT IN NORTH GEORGIA, THESIS, UNIVERSITY OF GEORGIA, 1936.

CURME, G. U. A GRAMMAR OF THE ENGLISH LANGUAGE, VOLS. II AND III, BOSTON, 1931, 1935.

CURME, G. O. PRINCIPLES AND PRACTICE OF ENGLISH GRAMMAR, NEW YORK, 1947.

CURTIS, J. F. AND HARDY, J. C. CITE IMPORTANCE TO THERAPY OF REGARDING PHONEME AS ARTICULATORY EVENT, FROM LETTERS TO THE EDITOR, JOURNAL OF SPEECH AND HEARING RESEARCH, IV, JUNE, 1961.

CUTTS, W. READING UNREADINESS IN THE UNDERPRIVILEGED, N. E. A. J., 1963, 52, 23–24.

D'ANGELO, R. A COMPARISON OF WHITE AND NEGRO PRE-SCHOOL CHILDREN IN GOODENOUGH, I. Q. AND LANGUAGE DEVELOPMENT, MASTER'S DISSERTATION, FORDHAM UNIVERSITY, 1950.

DAHLSTEDT, A. RHYTHM AND WORD ORDER IN ANGLO-SAXON AND SEMISAXON WITH SPECIAL REFERENCE TO THEIR DEVELOPMENT IN MODERN ENGLISH, E. MALMSTROM, LUND, SWEDEN, 1901.

DARLEY, F. L. AND WINITZ, H. AGE OF FIRST WORD, REVIEW OF RESEARCH, JOURNAL OF SPEECH AND HEARING DISORDERS, AUGUST, 1961, PP. 272–90.

DARWIN, C. DESCENT OF MAN, IN THE ORIGIN OF SPECIES AND THE DESCENT OF MAN, NEW YORK, RANDOM HOUSE.

DAVES, J. H. A SOCIAL STUDY OF THE COLORED POPULATION OF KNOXVILLE, TENNESSEE, KNOXVILLE, THE FREE COLORED LIBRARY, 1926.

DAVIS, A. L. A WORD ATLAS OF THE GREAT LAKES REGION, DOCTORAL DISSERTATION, UNIVERSITY OF MICHIGAN, 1948, MICROFILM.

DAVIS, A. L. AND McDAVID, R. I., JR. SHIVAREE, AN EXAMPLE OF CULTURAL DIFFUSION, AMERICAN SPEECH, XXIV (1949), 249–255.

DAVIS, A. SOCIAL-CLASS INFLUENCES UPON LEARNING, CAMBRIDGE, HARVARD UNIVERSITY PRESS, 1962.

DAVIS, A. TEACHING LANGUAGE AND READING TO DISADVANTAGED NEGRO CHILDREN, ELEMENTARY ENGLISH, 1965, 42, 791–797.

DAVIS, H. HEARING AND DEAFNESS, REVISED ED., NEW YORK, HOLT, RINEHART AND WINSTON, INC., 1960.

DAVIS, H., PETERSON, G. E. AND WEAVER, W. INFORMATION THEORY, JOURNAL OF SPEECH AND HEARING DISORDERS, XVII, JUNE, 1952, 166–97.

DAWE, H. A STUDY OF THE EFFECTS OF AN EDUCATIONAL PROGRAM UPON LANGUAGE DEVELOPMENT AND RELATED MENTAL FUNCTIONS IN YOUNG CHILDREN, JOURNAL OF EXPERIMENTAL EDUCATION, 1942, 11, 200–209.

DE FLEUR, M. L. AND LARSEN, O. L. THE FLOW OF INFORMATION, NEW YORK, HARPER AND ROW, PUBLISHERS, 1958.

DE GROTT, A. W. PHONETICS AND ITS RELATION TO AESTHETICS, MANUAL OF PHONETICS, L. KAISER, ED., AMSTERDAM, NORTH-HOLLAND PUBLISHING COMPANY, 1957.

DE SAUSSURE, F. COURSE IN GENERAL LINGUISTICS, NEW YORK, PHILOSOPHICAL LIBRARY, INC., 1959.

DEAN, L. F. AND WILSON, K. G. (EDS.) ESSAYS ON LANGUAGE AND USAGE, 2ND ED., NEW YORK, 1963.

DEBOER, J. J. SOME SOCIOLOGICAL FACTORS IN LANGUAGE DEVELOPMENT, ELEMENTARY ENGLISH, 1952, 29, 482–492.

DECAMP, D. THE PRONUNCIATION OF ENGLISH IN SAN FRANCISCO, ORBIS,

VII (JUNE, 1958), 372–391, VIII (JAN., 1959), 54–77.

DEUTSCH, M. THE DISADVANTAGED CHILD AND THE LEARNING PROCESS, PASSOW, A. H. (ED.), EDUCATION IN DEPRESSED AREAS, NEW YORK, T. C., COLUMBIA UNIVERSITY, 1963, PP. 163–180.

DEUTSCH, M. AND BROWN, B. SOCIAL INFLUENCES IN NEGRO-WHITE INTELLIGENCE DIFFERENCES, JOURNAL OF SOCIAL ISSUES, 1964, 20, 24–35.

DEUTSCH, M. THE ROLE OF SOCIAL CLASS IN LANGUAGE DEVELOPMENT AND COGNITION, AMERICAN JOURNAL OF ORTHOPSYCHIATRY, 1965, 25, 78–88.

DEUTSCH, M., MALIVER, A., BROWN, B., AND CHERRY, E. COMMUNICATION OF INFORMATION IN THE ELEMENTARY SCHOOL CLASSROOM, COOPERATIVE RESEARCH PROJECT NO. 908 OF THE OFFICE OF EDUCATION, E. S., DEPT. OF HEALTH, EDUCATION AND WELFARE, 1964.

DEXTER, E. A STUDY OF THE SPEECH DEVELOPMENT OF PRIMARY GRADE CHILDREN IN RELATION TO CERTAIN PERCEPTUAL, INTELLECTUAL, AND SOCIOLOGICAL FACTORS, DOCTORAL DISSERTATION, UNIVERSITY OF MICHIGAN (1961).

DILLARD, J. L. THE URBAN LANGUAGE STUDY OF THE CENTER FOR APPLIED LINGUISTICS, THE LINGUISTIC REPORTER, 1966, 8, 1–2.

DOBSON, E. J. ENGLISH PRONUNCIATION, 1500–1700, 2 VOLS. OXFORD, 1957.

DOLL, E. A. MEASUREMENT OF SOCIAL COMPETENCE, MINNEAPOLIS EDUCATIONAL TEST BUREAU, 1953.

DUCKERT, A. R. THE LINGUISTIC ATLAS OF NEW ENGLAND REVISITED, PUBLICATION OF THE AMERICAN DIALECT SOCIETY, NO. 39 (APRIL, 1963), PP.

DUNBAR, G. S. A SOUTHERN GEOGRAPHICAL WORD LIST, AMERICAN SPEECH, XXXVI (DEC., 1961), 293–296.

DUNN, H. L. COMMUNICATION AND PURPOSE-INGREDIENTS FOR LONGEVITY, JOURNAL OF SPEECH AND HEARING DISORDERS, XXVI, MAY, 1961, 109–17.

EDMONDS, W. SEX DIFFERENCES IN THE VERBAL ABILITY OF SOCIO-ECONOMICALLY DEPRESSED GROUPS, THE JOURNAL OF EDUCATIONAL RESEARCH, 1964., 58, 61–64.

EELLS, K. SOME IMPLICATIONS FOR SCHOOL PRACTICE OF THE CHICAGO STUDIES OF CULTURAL BIAS IN INTELLIGENCE TESTS, HARVARD EDUCATIONAL REVIEW, 1953, 23, 284–297.

EGEROD, S. THE LUNGTU DIALECT, A DESCRIPTION AND HISTORICAL STUDY OF A SOUTH CHINA IDIOM, ENJAR MUNKSGAARD LTD., COPENHAGEN, 1956.

EISENSON, J., AUER, J. J., IRWIN, D. V. THE PSYCHOLOGY OF COMMUNICATION, NEW YORK, APPLETON-CENTURY-CROFTS, 1963, PP. 141–59.

EKWALL, E. AMERICAN AND BRITISH PRONUNCIATION, UPSALA, 1946.

ELAM, S. ACCULTURATION AND LEARNING PROBLEMS OF PUERTO RICAN CHILDREN, TEACHERS COLLEGE RECORD, 1960, 61, 258–264.

ENGELMANN, S. CULTURAL DEPRI-

VATION AND REMEDY, INSTITUTE FOR RESEARCH ON EXCEPTIONAL CHILDREN, UNIVERSITY OF ILL., 1964.

ENGLISH SENTENCE PATTERN DRILLS FOR BEGINNING INDIAN CHILDREN, DIVISION OF INDIAN EDUCATION, NEW MEXICO STATE DEPARTMENT OF EDUCATION, SANTA FE, NEW MEXICO, 1962.

ENTWISLE, D. DEVELOPMENTAL SOCIOLINGUISTICS, A COMPARATIVE STUDY IN FOUR SUBCULTURAL SETTINGS, SOCIOMETRY, 1966, 29, 67–84.

ERVIN-TRIPP, S. AN ANALYSIS OF THE INTERACTION OF LANGUAGE, TOPIC AND LISTENER, IN J. J. GUMPERZ AND D. HYMES (EDS.), THE ETHNOGRAPHY OF COMMUNICATION, AMERICAN ANTHROPOLOGIST SPECIAL PUBLICATION, 1964, 66, NO. 6, PART 2.

EVANS, B. GRAMMAR FOR TODAY, INTRODUCTORY READINGS ON THE ENGLISH LANGUAGE, RICHARD BRADDOCK, ED., ENGLEWOOD CLIFFS, N. J., PRENTICE-HALL, INC., 1962.

FAIRBANKS, G. VOICE AND ARTICULATION DRILL BOOK, 2ND ED., NEW YORK, HARPER AND ROW, PUBLISHERS, INC., 1960.

FARR, T. J. THE LANGUAGE OF THE TENNESSEE MOUNTAIN REGIONS, AMERICAN SPEECH, XIV, 1939, PP. 89–92.

FERGUSON, C. A. DIGLOSSIA, WORD, 1959, 15, 325–340.

FINDLAY, D. C. AND McGUIRE, C. SOCIAL STATUS AND ABSTRACT BEHAVIOR, THE JOURNAL OF ABNORMAL AND SOCIAL PSYCHOLOGY, 1957, 54, 135–137.

FINOCCHIARO, M. TEACHING ENGLISH AS A SECOND LANGUAGE IN ELEMENTARY AND SECONDARY SCHOOLS, NEW YORK, HARPER AND ROW, PUBLISHERS, INC., 1958.

FIRTH, J. R. THE TONGUES OF MEN AND SPEECH, NEW YORK, 1964.

FISCHER-JORGENSEN, E. WHAT CAN THE NEW TECHNIQUES OF ACOUSTIC PHONETICS CONTRIBUTE TO LINGUISTICS, PSYCHOLINGUISTICS, SOL SAPORTA, ED., NEW YORK, HOLT, RINEHART AND WINSTON, INC., 1961.

FISCHER, J. L. SOCIAL INFLUENCES ON THE CHOICE OF A LINGUISTIC VARIANT IN D. HYMES (ED.), LANGUAGE IN CULTURE AND SOCIETY, A READER IN LINGUISTICS AND ANTHROPOLOGY, 1964, 483–488.

FLETCHER, S. G. SPEECH AS AN ELEMENT IN ORGANIZATION OF A MOTOR RESPONSE, JOURNAL OF SPEECH AND HEARING RESEARCH, 1962, PP. 292–99.

FLETCHER, H. AND STEINBERG, J. C. ARTICULATION TESTING METHODS, BELL SYSTEM TECHNICAL JOURNAL, VIII, 1929.

FLINT, K. D. ENGLISH FOR NEW AMERICANS, PHILADELPHIA, CHILTON COMPANY BOOK DIVISION, 1960.

FOGELQUIST, D. F. THE BILINGUALISM OF PARAGUAY, HISPANIA, XXXIII, 1950.

FOLLETT, W. MODERN AMERICAN USAGE, HILL AND WANG, NEW YORK, 1966.

FOLLET, W. BARGAIN BASEMENT ENGLISH, INTRODUCTORY READINGS ON THE ENGLISH LANGUAGE, RICHARD BRADDOCK, ED., ENGLEWOOD CLIFFS, N. J., PRENTICE-HALL, INC., 1962.

FORD, T. R., ED. THE SOUTHERN AP-

PALACHIAN REGION, A SURVEY, LEXINGTON, THE UNIVERSITY OF KENTUCKY PRESS, 1962.

FORUM, ASHA, V. APRIL, 1963, 616.

FOWLER, H. W. A DICTIONARY OF MODERN ENGLISH USAGE, OXFORD, 1926.

FRANCIS, W. N. THE STRUCTURE OF AMERICAN ENGLISH, NEW YORK, THE RONALD PRESS COMPANY, 1958.

FRAZIER, A. A RESEARCH PROPOSAL TO DEVELOP THE LANGUAGE SKILLS OF CHILDREN WITH POOR BACKGROUNDS, IN A. JEWETT, J. MERSARD, AND D. GUNDERSOND (EDS.), IMPROVING ENGLISH SKILLS OF CULTURALLY DIFFERENT YOUTH, WASHINGTON, D. C., U. S. GOVERNMENT PRINTING OFFICE, 1964.

FRIES, C. C. AMERICAN ENGLISH GRAMMAR, APPLETON - CENTURY - CROFTS, NEW YORK, 1940.

FRIES, C. C. THE STRUCTURE OF ENGLISH, HARCOURT, BRACE AND WORLD, NEW YORK, 1952.

FRIES, C. AN INTENSIVE COURSE IN ENGLISH FOR LATIN-AMERICAN STUDENTS, ANN ARBOR, MICH., ENGLISH LANGUAGE INSTITUTE, UNIVERSITY OF MICH. PRESS, 1947.

FRIES, C. MEANING AND LINGUISTIC ANALYSIS, READINGS IN APPLIED LINGUISTICS, H. B. ALLEN, ED., NEW YORK, APPLETON-CENTURY-CROFTS, 1958.

FRY, D. B. PERCEPTION AND RECOGNITION IN SPEECH, FOR ROMAN JAKOBSON, MORRIS HALLE, ET AL., EDS., THE HAGUE, MOUTON AND COMPANY, 1956.

GLANZER, M. TOWARD A PSYCHOLOGY OF LANGUAGE STRUCTURE, JOURNAL OF SPEECH AND HEARING RESEARCH, V, DECEMBER, 1962.

GLEASON, H. A., JR. LINGUISTICS AND ENGLISH GRAMMAR, HOLT, RINEHART AND WINSTON, NEW YORK, 1965.

GOLDFARB, W. THE EFFECTS OF PSYCHOLOGICAL DEPRIVATION IN INFANCY AND SUBSEQUENT STIMULATION, AMERICAN JOURNAL OF PSYCHIATRY, 1945, 102, 18–33.

GORDON, M. J. AND WONG, H. H. A MANUAL FOR SPEECH IMPROVEMENT, ENGLEWOOD CLIFFS, N. J., PRENTICE-HALL, INC., 1961.

GRAY, G. W. AND WISE, C. M. THE BASES OF SPEECH, 3RD ED., NEW YORK, HARPER AND ROW, PUBLISHERS, 1959.

GRAY, S., KLAUS, R., MILLER, J., AND FORRESTER, B. BEFORE FIRST GRADE, NEW YORK, TEACHERS COLLEGE PRESS, 1966.

GREENOUGH, J. B. AND KITTREDGE, G. L. WORDS AND THEIR WAYS IN ENGLISH SPEECH, NEW YORK, 1901.

GREEN, E. YIDDISH AND ENGLISH IN DETROIT, A SURVEY AND ANALYSIS OF RECIPROCAL INFLUENCES IN BILINGUALS' PRONUNCIATION, GRAMMAR, AND VOCABULARY, DOCTORAL DISSERTATION, UNIVERSITY OF MICHIGAN (1962).

GREEN, G. SECTION B, NEGRO DIALECT, THE LAST BARRIER TO INTEGRATION, JOURNAL OF NEGRO EDUCATION, 1962, 31, 81–83.

GREEN, W. LANGUAGE AND THE CULTURALLY DIFFERENT, ENGLISH JOURNAL, 1965, 54, 724–733.

GROPPER, G., HOLLAND, A., LIEBERGOTT, J., AND SHORT,

J. INVESTIGATION OF SPEECH PROB-
LEMS AMONG JOB CORPSMEN, AMERI-
CAN INSTITUTES FOR RESEARCH, 1967.

GUMPERZ, J. J. TYPES OF LINGUISTIC
COMMUNITIES, ANTHROPOLOGICAL
LINGUISTICS, 1962, 4, 28–40.

GUMPERZ, J. J. AND HYMES, D.
THE ETHNOGRAPHY OF COMMUNICA-
TION, AMERICAN ANTHROPOLOGIST
SPECIAL PUBLICATION, 1964, 66, NO.
6, (WHOLE PART 2) .

HADDING-KOCH, K. ACOUSTICO-
PHONETIC STUDIES IN THE INTONA-
TION OF SOUTHERN SWEDISH, C. W. K.
GLEERUP, LUND, SWEDEN, 1961.

HALL, E. THE SILENT LANGUAGE, GAR-
DEN CITY, N. Y., DOUBLEDAY AND
COMPANY, INC., 1959.

HALL, J. S. THE PHONETICS OF GREAT
SMOKY MOUNTAIN SPEECH, AMERI-
CAN SPEECH REPRINTS AND MONO-
GRAPHS, NO. 4., NEW YORK, KING'S
CROWN PRESS, 1942.

HALL, M. E. AUDITORY FACTORS IN
FUNCTIONAL ARTICULATORY SPEECH
DEFECTS, DOCTORAL DISSERTATION,
STATE UNIVERSITY OF IOWA, 1936,
JOURNAL OF EXPERIMENTAL EDUCA-
TION, VII, 1933–1939.

HALL, R. A., JR. LINGUISTICS AND
YOUR LANGUAGE, REV. ED., NEW
YORK, DOUBLEDAY AND COMPANY,
INC., 1960.

HALL, R. A., JR. THE AFRICAN SUB-
STRATUM IN NEGRO ENGLISH, AMERI-
CAN SPEECH, 25, 1950, PP. 51–54.

HANKEY, C. T. SEMANTIC FEATURES
AND EASTERN RELICS IN COLORADO
DIALECT, AMERICAN SPEECH, XXXVI
(DEC., 1961) , 266–270.

HANKEY, C. T. A COLORADO WORD
GEOGRAPHY, PUBLICATION OF THE

AMERICAN DIALECT SOCIETY, NO. 34
(NOV., 1960) .

HANLEY, T. D. AND THURMAN,
W. L. DEVELOPING VOCAL SKILLS,
NEW YORK, HOLT, RINEHART AND
WINSTON, INC., 1962.

HANLEY, T. D. AND THURMAN,
W. L. STUDENT PROJECTS FOR DE-
VELOPING VOCAL SKILLS, NEW YORK,
HOLT, RINEHART AND WINSTON, INC.,
1962.

HANSEN, B. F. THE APPLICATION OF
SOUND DISCRIMINATION TESTS TO
FUNCTIONAL ARTICULATORY DEFECTS,
UNPUBLISHED MASTER'S THESIS, PUR-
DUE UNIVERSITY, 1942.

HARMS, L. S. LISTENER COMPREHEN-
SION OF SPEAKERS OF THREE STATUS
GROUPS, LANGUAGE AND SPEECH,
1961, 4, 109–112.

HARMS, L. S. LISTENER JUDGEMENTS
OF STATUS CUES IN SPEECH, QUARTER-
LY JOURNAL OF SPEECH, 1961, 47,
164–168.

HARMS, L. S. STATUS CUES IN SPEECH
EXTRA-RACE AND EXTRA-REGION IDEN-
TIFICATION, LINGUA, 1963, 12, 300–
306.

HARMS, L. S. PROGRAMMED LEARN-
ING FOR THE FIELD OF SPEECH, THE
SPEECH TEACHER, X, SEPTEMBER,
1961.

HARRIS, J. W. THE DIALECT OF AP-
PALACHIA IN SOUTHERN ILLINOIS,
AMERICAN SPEECH, XXI, 1946, PP. 96–
99.

HARRIS, Z. S. STRUCTURAL LINGUIS-
TICS, CHICAGO, 1960.

HATCHER, J. W. APPALACHIAN
AMERICA, COUCH, W. T., ED., CULTURE
IN THE SOUTH, CHAPEL HILL UNIVER-

SITY OF NORTH CAROLINA PRESS, 1934.

HATTORI, S. THE ANALYSIS OF MEANING FOR ROMAN JAKOBSON, THE HAGUE, MOUTON AND COMPANY, 1956.

HAUGEN, E. THE BILINGUAL COMMUNITY, BILINGUALISM IN THE AMERICAS, A BIBLIOGRAPHY AND RESEARCH GUIDE, PUBLICATION OF THE AMERICAN DIALECT SOCIETY, NO. 26, UNIVERSITY OF ALABAMA PRESS, UNIVERSITY, ALABAMA, 1956.

HAUGEN, E. THE BILINGUAL INDIVIDUAL, PSYCHOLINGUISTICS, SOL SAPORTA, ED., NEW YORK, HOLT, RINEHART AND WINSTON, INC., 1961.

HAUGEN, E. LANGUAGE IN CONTACT, PROCEEDINGS OF THE VIII INTERNATIONAL CONGRESS OF LINGUISTS, OSLO, OSLO UNIVERSITY PRESS, 1958.

HEFFNER, R-M. S. GENERAL PHONETICS, MADISON, WIS., THE UNIVERSITY OF WIS. PRESS, 1952.

HERMAN, S. EXPLORATIONS IN THE SOCIAL PSYCHOLOGY OF LANGUAGE, CHOICE HUMAN RELATIONS, 1961, 12, 149–164.

HERTZLER, J. A SOCIOLOGY OF LANGUAGE, NEW YORK, RANDOM HOUSE, 1965.

HESS, R. D. EDUCABILITY AND REHABILITATION, THE FUTURE OF THE WELFARE CLASS, JOURNAL OF MARRIAGE AND THE FAMILY, 1964, 26, 422–429.

HESS, R. D. AND SHIPMAN, V. EARLY BLOCKS TO CHILDREN'S LEARNING, CHILDREN, 1965, 12, 189–194.

HESS, R. D. AND SHIPMAN, V. EARLY EXPERIENCE AND THE SOCIALIZATION OF COGNITIVE MODES IN CHIL-DREN, CHILD DEVELOPMENT, 1965, 36, 869–886.

HIBBEN, F. THE LOST AMERICANS, NEW YORK, THE CROWELL-COLLIER PUBLISHING CO., 1961.

HIBLER, M. A. A COMPARATIVE STUDY OF SPEECH PATTERNS OF SELECTED NEGRO AND WHITE KINDERGARTEN CHILDREN, DOCTORAL DISSERTATION, UNIVERSITY OF SOUTHERN CALIFORNIA, 1960.

HIGGINS, C. AND SIVERS, C. A COMPARISON OF STANFORD-BINET AND COLORED RAVEN PROGRESSIVE MATRICES IQS FOR CHILDREN WITH LOW SOCIOECONOMIC STATUS, JOURNAL OF CONSULTING PSYCHOLOGY, 1958, 22, 465–468.

HILL, E. H. AND GIAMMATTEO, M. C. SOCIO-ECONOMIC STATUS AND ITS RELATIONSHIP TO SCHOOL ACHIEVEMENT IN THE ELEMENTARY SCHOOL, ELEMENTARY ENGLISH, 1963, 40, 265–270.

HOCKETT, C. F. AGE-GRADING AND LINGUISTIC CONTINUITY, LANGUAGE, 1950, 26, 449–457.

HOCKETT, C. A COURSE IN MODERN LINGUISTICS, NEW YORK, THE MACMILLAN COMPANY, 1958.

HOCKETT, C. LOGICAL CONSIDERATIONS IN THE STUDY OF ANIMAL COMMUNICATION IN ANIMAL SOUNDS AND COMMUNICATION, W. E. LANYON AND W. N. TAVOLGA, EDS., WASHINGTON, D. C., PUBLICATION NO. 7, AMERICAN INSTITUTE OF BIOLOGICAL SCIENCE, 1960, PP. 392–427.

HOCKETT, C. IDIOM FORMATION FOR ROMAN JAKOBSON, THE HAGUE, MOUTON AND COMPANY, 1956.

HOLBROOK, A. AND FAIRBANKS, G. DIPHTHONG FORMANTS AND THEIR MOVEMENTS, JOURNAL OF SPEECH AND HEARING RESEARCH, V, MARCH, 1962.

HOLLIEN, H. AND MALCIK, E. ADOLESCENT VOICE CHANGE IN SOUTHERN NEGRO MALES, SPEECH MONOGRAPHS, VOL. 26, 1 (1962).

HORNSBY, A. S., GATENBY, E. V., AND WAKEFIELD, H. ADVANCED LEARNER'S DICTIONARY OF CURRENT ENGLISH, NEW YORK, OXFORD UNIVERSITY PRESS, 1960.

HUBBELL, A. F. THE PRONUNCIATION OF ENGLISH IN NEW YORK CITY, NEW YORK, KINGS CROWN PRESS, 1950.

HUBBELL, A. F. THE PHONEMIC ANALYSIS OF UNSTRESSED VOWELS, AMERICAN SPEECH, XXV, 1950.

HUGHES, J. P. THE SCIENCE OF LANGUAGE, NEW YORK, RANDOM HOUSE, INC., 1962.

HULTZEN, L. S. PHONETICS, PHONEMES AND TEACHERS OF SPEECH, QUARTERLY JOURNAL OF SPEECH, APRIL, 1949, PP. 202–5.

HUMPHREY, W. R. AND MILISEN, R. A STUDY OF THE ABILITY TO REPRODUCE UNFAMILIAR SOUNDS WHICH HAVE BEEN PRESENTED ORALLY, JOURNAL OF SPEECH AND HEARING DISORDERS, MONOGRAPH SUPPLEMENT, NO. 4, DECEMBER, 1954.

HUNT, J. THE PSYCHOLOGICAL BASIS FOR USING PRESCHOOL ENRICHMENT AS AN ANTIDOTE FOR CULTURAL DEPRIVATION, MERRILL-PALMER QUARTERLY, 1964, 10, 209–248.

HYMES, D. THE ETHNOGRAPHY OF SPEAKING IN THE ANTHROPOLOGICAL SOCIETY OF WASHINGTON, ANTHROPOLOGY AND HUMAN BEHAVIOR, WASHINGTON, D. C., AUTHOR, 1962, 13–53.

HYMES, D. DIRECTIONS IN (ETHNO-) LINGUISTIC THEORY, IN A. K. ROMNEY AND F. G. D'ANDRADE (EDS.), TRANSCULTURAL STUDIES IN COGNITION, AMERICAN ANTHROPOLOGIST SPECIAL PUBLICATION, 1964, 66, NO. 3, PART 2, 6–56.

HYMES, D. INTRODUCTION TOWARD ETHNOGRAPHIES OF COMMUNICATION, IN J. J. GUMPERZ AND D. HYMES (EDS.), THE ETHNOGRAPHY OF COMMUNICATION, AMERICAN ANTHROPOLOGIST SPECIAL PUBLICATION, 1964, 66, NO. 6, PART 2, 1–34.

HYMES, D. THE ANTHROPOLOGY OF COMMUNICATION, IN F. E. X. DANCE (ED.), HUMAN COMMUNICATION THEORY, NEW YORK, HOLT, RINEHART AND WINSTON, 1967, 1–39.

IRWIN, O. C. INFANT SPEECH THE EFFECT OF FAMILY OCCUPATIONAL STATUS AND OF AGE ON SOUND FREQUENCY, JOURNAL OF SPEECH AND HEARING DISORDERS, 1948, 13, 320–323.

IRWIN, O. C. SPEECH DEVELOPMENT IN THE YOUNG CHILD 2. SOME FACTORS RELATED TO THE SPEECH DEVELOPMENT OF THE INFANT AND YOUNG CHILD, JOURNAL OF SPEECH AND HEARING DISORDERS, 1952, 17, 269–278.

IRWIN, O. INFANT SPEECH EFFECT OF SYSTEMATIC READING OF STORIES, JOURNAL OF SPEECH AND HEARING RESEARCH, III, JUNE, 1960, 187–90.

IRWIN, O. AND CHEN, H. P. INFANT SPEECH VOWEL AND CONSONANT FRE-

QUENCY, JOURNAL OF SPEECH AND HEARING DISORDERS, XI, JUNE, 1946, 123-25.

JACKSON, E. H. AN ANALYSIS OF CERTAIN COLORADO ATLAS FIELD RECORDS WITH REGARD TO SETTLEMENT HISTORY AND OTHER FACTORS, DOCTORAL DISSERTATION, UNIVERSITY OF COLORADO, 1956, MICROFILM.

JENKINS, J. J. AND PALERMO, D. S. MEDIATION PROCESSES AND THE ACQUISITION OF LINGUISTIC STRUCTURE, BELLUGI, U. AND BROWN, R., EDS., THE ACQUISITION OF LANGUAGE. MONOGR. SOC. RES. CHILD DEVELOPMENT, 1964, 29, 141-169.

JESPERSEN, O. ESSENTIALS OF ENGLISH GRAMMAR, HENRY HOLT, NEW YORK, 1933.

JESPERSEN, O. GROWTH AND STRUCTURE OF THE ENGLISH LANGUAGE, 9TH ED., OXFORD, BLACKWELL, 1952.

JOHNSON, F. C. AND FRANDSEN, K. ADMINISTERING THE BROWN-CARLSEN LISTENING COMPREHENSION TEST, THE JOURNAL OF COMMUNICATION, XVIII, MARCH, 1963.

JOHNSON, W. PEOPLE IN QUANDARIES, NEW YORK, HARPER AND ROW, PUBLISHERS, 1949.

JOHNSON, W. THE ONSET OF STUTTERING, MINNEAPOLIS, UNIVERSITY OF MINN. PRESS, 1959.

JOHN, V. THE INTELLECTUAL DEVELOPMENT OF SLUM CHILDREN SOME PRELIMINARY FINDINGS, AMERICAN JOURNAL OF ORTHOPSYCHIATRY, 1963, 33, 813-822.

JOHN, V. P. AND GOLDSTEIN, L. S. THE SOCIAL CONTEXT OF LANGUAGE ACQUISITION, MERRILL-PAL-MER QUARTERLY, 1964, 10, 265-275.

JONES, D. AN ENGLISH PRONOUNCING DICTIONARY, 12TH ED., LONDON, 1963.

JONES, D. THE PRONUNCIATION OF ENGLISH, 4TH ED., THE UNIVERSITY PRESS, CAMBRIDGE, ENG., 1958.

JONES, D. AN OUTLINE OF ENGLISH PHONETICS, 3RD ED., DUTTON, NEW YORK, 1932.

JONES, D. AN OUTLINE OF ENGLISH PHONETICS, 9TH ED., W. H. HEFFER AND SONS, CAMBRIDGE, ENGLAND, 1962.

JONES, D. THE PRONUNCIATION OF ENGLISH, 3RD ED., CAMBRIDGE, ENGLAND, THE UNIVERSITY PRESS, 1950.

JOOS, M. ACOUSTIC PHONETICS, BALTIMORE, WAVERLY PRESS, 1948, LANGUAGE MONOGRAPH 23.

JOOS, M. ACOUSTIC PHONETICS, LANGUAGE MONOGRAPH 23, BALTIMORE, WAVERLY PRESS, 1948.

JOOS, M. DESCRIPTION OF LANGUAGE DESIGN, JOURNAL OF THE ACOUSTICAL SOCIETY OF AMERICA, XXII, 1950.

JOOS, M. SEMOLOGY, A LINGUISTIC THEORY OF MEANING, STUDIES IN LINGUISTICS, XIII, WINTER, 1958.

KAISER, L. ED. MANUAL OF PHONETICS, AMSTERDAM, NORTH-HOLLAND PUBLISHING COMPANY, 1957.

KANTNER, C. AND WEST, R. PHONETICS, REV. ED., NEW YORK, HARPER AND ROW, PUBLISHERS, 1960.

KANTNER, C. E. AND WEST, R. PHONETICS, REV. ED., NEW YORK, HARPER AND ROW, PUBLISHERS, INC., 1960.

KAPLAN, H. M. ANATOMY AND PHY-

SIOLOGY OF SPEECH, NEW YORK, MC-GRAW-HILL BOOK COMPANY, 1960.

KEENAN, J. S. WHAT IS MEDIAL POSITION, JOURNAL OF SPEECH AND HEARING DISORDERS, XXVI, MAY, 1961.

KELLER, S. THE SOCIAL WORLD OF THE URBAN SLUM CHILD, SOME EARLY FINDINGS, AMERICAN JOURNAL OF ORTHOPSYCHIATRY, 33, 823–831, (1963).

KELLMER PRINGLE, M. L. AND BOSSIO, V. A STUDY OF DEPRIVED CHILDREN, PART II, LANGUAGE DEVELOPMENT AND READING ATTAINMENT, VITA HUMANA, 1958, 1, 142–170.

KELLMER PRINGLE, M. L. AND TANNER, M. THE EFFECTS OF EARLY DEPRIVATION ON SPEECH DEVELOPMENT, A COMPARATIVE STUDY OF 4 YEAR OLDS IN A NURSERY SCHOOL AND IN RESIDENTIAL NURSERIES, LANGUAGE AND SPEECH, 1958, 1, 269–287.

KELLOG, W. N. AND KELLOG, L. A. THE APES AND THE CHILD, NEW YORK, MCGRAW-HILL BOOK COMPANY, 1953.

KENNEDY, A. G. CURRENT ENGLISH, BOSTON, 1935.

KENNEDY, A. G. ENGLISH USAGE, A STUDY IN POLICY AND PROCEDURE, NEW YORK, 1942.

KENYON, J. S. AMERICAN PRONUNCIATION, 10TH ED., ANN ARBOR, MICHIGAN: GEORGE WAHR, PUBLISHER, 1961.

KENYON, J. S. AND KNOTT, T. A. A PRONOUNCING DICTIONARY OF AMERICAN ENGLISH, SPRINGFIELD, MASS., G. AND C. MERRIAM COMPANY, 1944.

KENYON, J. S. AMERICAN PRONUN-

CIATION, ANN ARBOR, MICH., GEORGE WAHR, PUBLISHER, 1946.

KENYON, J. S. AND KNOTT, T. A. A PRONOUNCING DICTIONARY OF AMERICAN ENGLISH, SPRINGFIELD, MASS., G. AND C. MERRIAM COMPANY, 1944.

KEPHART, H. OUR SOUTHERN HIGHLANDERS, NEW YORK, OUTING PUBLISHING COMPANY, 1913.

KERR, E. M. AND ADERMAN, R. M. ASPECTS OF AMERICAN ENGLISH, NEW YORK, HARCOURT, BRACE AND WORLD, INC., 1963.

KHATER, M. R. THE INFLUENCE OF SOCIAL CLASS ON THE LANGUAGE PATTERNS OF KINDERGARTEN CHILDREN, UNPUBLISHED DOCTORAL DISSERTATION, UNIVERSITY OF CHICAGO, 1951.

KIMMERLE, M. M., McDAVID, R. I., AND McDAVID, V. G. PROBLEMS OF LINGUISTIC GEOGRAPHY IN THE ROCKY MOUNTAIN AREA, WESTERN HUMANITIES REVIEW, V (SUMMER, 1951), 249–264.

KINGDON, R. TONETIC STRESS MARKERS FOR ENGLISH, LE MAITRE PHONETIQUE, 3.54, 60–64, 1939.

KINGDON, R. THE GROUNDWORK OF ENGLISH INTONATION, LONGMANS, GREEN AND CO., LONDON, NEW YORK, AND TORONTO, 1958.

KLIMA, E. S. RELATEDNESS BETWEEN GRAMMATICAL SYSTEMS LANGUAGE, 1964, 40, 1–20.

KLIMA, E. S. NEGATION IN ENGLISH, IN THE STRUCTURE OF LANGUAGE, J. J. FODOR AND J. A. KATZ, EDS., PRENTICE-HALL, ENGLEWOOD CLIFFS, N. J., 1964.

KLINGER, H. IMITATED ENGLISH CLEFT PALATE SPEECH IN A NORMAL

SPANISH SPEAKING CHILD, JOURNAL OF SPEECH AND HEARING DISORDERS, XXVII, NOVEMBER, 1962, 379–81.

KOHLER, W. THE MENTALITY OF APES, NEW YORK, HARCOURT, BRACE AND WORLD, INC., 1925.

KRASNER, L. STUDIES OF THE CONDITIONING OF VERBAL BEHAVIOR, PSYCHOLINGUISTICS, SOL SAPORTA, ED., NEW YORK, HOLT, RINEHART AND WINSTON, INC., 1961.

KRUGMAN, M. THE CULTURALLY DEPRIVED CHILD IN SCHOOL, NATIONAL EDUCATION ASSOCIATION JOURNAL, 1961, 50, 23–24.

KURATH, H. HANDBOOK OF THE LINGUISTIC GEOGRAPHY OF NEW ENGLAND, PROVIDENCE, BROWN UNIVERSITY PRESS, 1939.

KURATH, H. DIALECT AREAS, SETTLEMENT AREAS AND CULTURAL AREAS IN THE UNITED STATES, CULTURAL APPROACH TO HISTORY, ED. C. F. WARE, NEW YORK, COLUMBIA UNIVERSITY PRESS, 1940, PP. 331–351.

KURATH, H. A WORD GEOGRAPHY OF THE EASTERN UNITED STATES, ANN ARBOR, UNIVERSITY OF MICHIGAN PRESS, 1949.

KURATH, H., KUHN, S. M., AND OTHERS (ED.) MIDDLE ENGLISH DICTIONARY, ANN ARBOR, MICH., 1952.

KURATH, H. A WORD GEOGRAPHY OF THE EASTERN UNITED STATES, ANN ARBOR, MICHIGAN, 1949.

KURATH, H. ET AL. HANDBOOK OF THE LINGUISTIC GEOGRAPHY OF NEW ENGLAND, PROVIDENCE, R. I., 1939.

KURATH, H. ET AL. LINGUISTIC ATLAS OF NEW ENGLAND, PROVIDENCE, R. I., 1939–43.

KURATH, H. AND McDAVID, R. I.,

JR. THE PRONUNCIATION OF ENGLISH IN THE ATLANTIC STATES, UNIVERSITY OF MICHIGAN STUDIES IN AMERICAN ENGLISH, NO. 3, ANN ARBOR, MICHIGAN, 1961.

LABOV, W. THE SOCIAL MOTIVATION OF A SOUND CHANGE, WORD XIX (DEC., 1963), 273–309.

LABOV, W. A PRELIMINARY STUDY OF THE STRUCTURE OF ENGLISH USED BY NEGRO AND PUERTO RICAN SPEAKERS IN NEW YORK CITY, COOPERATIVE RESEARCH PROJECT NO. 3091, U. S. DEPARTMENT OF HEALTH, EDUCATION AND WELFARE, WASHINGTON, D. C., 1965.

LABOV, W. STAGES IN THE ACQUISITION OF STANDARD ENGLISH, IN R. W. SHUY (ED.), SOCIAL DIALECTS AND LANGUAGE LEARNING, CHAMPAIGN-URBANA NATIONAL COUNCIL OF TEACHERS OF ENGLISH, 1965, 77–103.

LACIVITA, A., KEAN, J. M., AND YAMAMOTO, K. SOCIO-ECONOMIC STATUS OF CHILDREN AND ACQUISITION OF GRAMMAR, THE JOURNAL OF EDUCATIONAL RESEARCH, 1966, 60, 71–74.

LADO, R. LINGUISTICS ACROSS CULTURES APPLIED LINGUISTICS FOR LANGUAGE TEACHERS, ANN ARBOR, UNIVERSITY OF MICHIGAN PRESS, 1957.

LADO, R. LANGUAGE TEACHING, NEW YORK, McGRAW-HILL BOOK COMPANY, 1964.

LADO, R. LANGUAGE TESTING, NEW YORK, LONGMANS, GREEN AND COMPANY, INC., 1961.

LAMBERT, W. E. PSYCHOLOGICAL APPROACHES TO THE STUDY OF LANGUAGE, PART II ON SECOND-LANGUAGE LEARNING AND BILINGUALISM, THE

MODERN LANGUAGE JOURNAL, 1963, 47, 114–121.

LAMBERT, W. E. AND FILLEN-BAUM, S. A PILOT STUDY OF APHASIA AMONG BILINGUALS, PSYCHOLINGUISTICS, SOL SAPORTA, ED., NEW YORK, HOLT, RINEHART AND WINSTON, INC., 1961.

LANE, H. SOME DIFFERENCES IN FIRST AND SECOND LANGUAGE LEARNING, LANGUAGE LEARNING, XII, 1962.

LANE, H. AND MOORE, D. J. RECONDITIONING A CONSONANT DISCRIMINATION IN AN APHASIC, JOURNAL OF SPEECH AND HEARING DISORDERS, XXVII, AUGUST, 1962.

LANGDON-DAVIES, J. ON THE NATURE OF MAN, NEW YORK, NEW AMERICAN LIBRARY OF WORLD LITERATURE, INC., 1961.

LANGER, S. PHILOSOPHY IN A NEW KEY, 2ND ED., NEW YORK, THE NEW AMERICAN LIBRARY OF WORLD LITERATURE, INC., 1961.

LANGER, S. SPEECH AND ITS COMMUNICATIVE FUNCTION, QUARTERLY JOURNAL OF SPEECH, XLVI, 1946.

LARSON, R. AND OLSON, J. L. A METHOD OF IDENTIFYING CULTURALLY DEPRIVED KINDERGARTEN CHILDREN, EXCEPTIONAL CHILDREN, 1963, 30, 130–134.

LAWTON, D. SOCIAL CLASS LANGUAGE DIFFERENCES IN GROUP DISCUSSIONS, LANGUAGE AND SPEECH, 1964, 7, 183–204.

LAWTON, D. SOCIAL CLASS DIFFERENCES IN LANGUAGE DEVELOPMENT A STUDY OF SOME SAMPLES OF WRITTEN WORK, LANGUAGE AND SPEECH, 1963, 6, 120–142.

LEES, R. B. THE GRAMMAR OF ENGLISH NOMINALIZATIONS, BLOOMINGTON, INDIANA, 1960.

LEE, D. W. FUNCTIONAL CHANGE IN EARLY ENGLISH, MENASHA, WISCONSIN, 1948.

LEE, I. J. LANGUAGE HABITS IN HUMAN AFFAIRS, NEW YORK, HARPER AND ROW, PUBLISHERS, INC., 1941.

LEE, L. DEVELOPMENTAL SENTENCE TYPES A METHOD FOR COMPARING NORMAL AND DEVIANT SYNTACTIC DEVELOPMENT, JOURNAL OF SPEECH AND HEARING RESEARCH, 1966, 31, 311-330.

LEMERT, E. M. SOME INDIANS WHO STUTTER, JOURNAL OF SPEECH AND HEARING DISORDERS, XVIII, 1953, NO. 2, 168–74.

LENTZ, L. B. AND SHERMAN, D. PHONETIC ELEMENTS AND PERCEPTION OF NASALITY, JOURNAL OF SPEECH AND HEARING RESEARCH, IV, DECEMBER, 1961.

LEONARD, S. A. THE DOCTRINE OF CORRECTNESS IN ENGLISH USAGE, 1700–1800 UNIVERSITY OF WISCONSIN STUDIES IN LANGUAGE AND LITERATURE, NO. 25. MADISON, WISCONSIN, 1929.

LERMAN, P. ARGOT, SYMBOLIC DEVIANCE AND SUBCULTURAL DELINQUENCY, AMERICAN SOCIOLOGICAL REVIEW, 1967, 32, 209–224.

LEUTENEGGER, R. R. THE SOUNDS OF AMERICAN ENGLISH AN INTRODUCTION TO PHONETICS, CHICAGO, SCOTT, FORESMAN AND COMPANY, 1963.

LEWIS, M. M. INFANT SPEECH, LONDON, ROUTLEDGE AND KEGAN PAUL, LTD., 1936.

LINTON, L. AN EXPERIMENTAL STUDY

OF SPEECH SOUND DISCRIMINATION, UNPUBLISHED MASTER'S THESIS, LELAND, STANFORD JUNIOR UNIVERSITY, 1939.

LLOYD, D. J. AND WARFEL, H. R. AMERICAN ENGLISH IN ITS CULTURAL SETTING, NEW YORK, 1956.

LOBAN, W. LANGUAGE PROFICIENCY AND SCHOOL LEARNING, IN J. D. KRUMBOLTZ (ED), LEARNING AND THE EDUCATIONAL PROCESS, CHICAGO, RAND MCNALLY, 1965, 113–131.

LOBAN, W. A SUSTAINED PROGRAM OF LANGUAGE LEARNING, IN R. CORBIN AND M. CROSBY (EDS.), LANGUAGE PROGRAMS FOR THE DISADVANTAGED CHAMPAIGN, ILL., NATIONAL COUNCIL OF TEACHERS OF ENGLISH, 1965.

LOTZ, J. ON THE LINGUISTIC STRUCTURE OF SPEECH, LOGOS, VI, APRIL, 1963.

MALLERY, G. SIGN LANGUAGE AMONG NORTH AMERICAN INDIANS FIRST ANNUAL REPORT OF THE BUREAU OF ETHNOLOGY, SMITHSONIAN INSTITUTION, I (1881), 279–89.

MALONE, K. THE PHONEMES OF CURRENT ENGLISH, STUDIES IN HEROIC LEGEND AND IN CURRENT SPEECH, PP. 226–67. COPENHAGEN, 1959.

MANSER, R. B. SPEECH CORRECTION ON THE CONTRACT PLAN, ENGLEWOOD CLIFFS, N. J., PRENTICE-HALL, INC. 1951.

MARCKWARDT, A. H. MIDDLE ENGLISH O IN AMERICAN ENGLISH OF THE GREAT LAKES AREA, PAPERS OF THE MICHIGAN ACADEMY OF SCIENCE, XXVI (1941), 561–571.

MARCKWARDT, A. H. MIDDLE ENGLISH WA IN THE SPEECH OF THE GREAT LAKES REGION, AMERICAN SPEECH, XVII (DEC., 1942), 226–234.

MARCKWARDT, A. H. PRINCIPAL AND SUBSIDIARY DIALECT AREAS IN THE NORTH-CENTRAL STATES, PUBLICATION OF THE AMERICAN DIALECT SOCIETY, NO. 27 (1957), PP. 3–15.

MARCKWARDT, A. H. AMERICAN ENGLISH, NEW YORK, OXFORD UNIVERSITY PRESS, INC., 1958.

MARCKWARDT, A. H. AND WALCOTT, F. G. FACTS ABOUT CURRENT ENGLISH USAGE, NEW YORK, 1938.

MARGE, M. THE INFLUENCE OF SELECTED HOME BACKGROUND VARIABLES ON THE DEVELOPMENT OF ORAL COMMUNICATION SKILLS IN CHILDREN, JOURNAL OF SPEECH AND HEARING RESEARCH, 1965, 8, 291–309.

MARLAND, P. SHADOWING—A CONTRIBUTION TO THE TREATMENT OF STAMMERING, FOLIA PHONETICA, IX, 1957.

MATTHEWS, E. M. NEIGHBOR AND KIN LIFE IN A TENNESSEE RIDGE COMMUNITY, NASHVILLE, VANDERBILT UNIVERSITY PRESS, 1965.

MATTHIAS, V. P. FOLK SPEECH OF PINE MOUNTAIN, KENTUCKY, AMERICAN SPEECH XXI, 1946, PP. 188–192.

MAY, F. THE EFFECTS OF ENVIRONMENT OF ORAL LANGUAGE DEVELOPMENT, ELEMENTARY ENGLISH, 1966, 43, 720–729.

McCARTHY, D. THE LANGUAGE DEVELOPMENT OF THE PRESCHOOL CHILD, THE INSTITUTE OF CHILD WELFARE MONOGRAPH SERIES, 1930, NO. 4.

McCARTHY, D. FACTORS THAT INFLUENCE LANGUAGE GROWTH HOME

INFLUENCES, ELEMENTARY ENGLISH, 1952, 29, 421–428, 440.

McCARTHY, D. LANGUAGE DISORDERS AND PARENT-CHILD RELATIONSHIP, JOURNAL OF SPEECH AND HEARING DISORDERS, 1954, 19, 514–523.

McCARTHY, D. LANGUAGE DEVELOPMENT IN CHILDREN, IN L. CARMICHAEL (ED), MANUAL OF CHILD PSYCHOLOGY, NEW YORK, N. Y. 1954, WILEY.

McDAVID, R. I., JR. LINGUISTIC GEOGRAPHY IN CANADA, AN INTRODUCTION, JOURNAL OF THE CANADIAN LINGUISTIC ASSOCIATION, I, 1 (OCT., 1954), 3–8.

McDAVID, R. I., JR. AND McDAVID, V. G. GRAMMATICAL DIFFERENCES IN THE NORTH CENTRAL STATES, AMERICAN SPEECH, XXXV (FEB., 1960) 5–19.

McDAVID, R. I., JR. AND McDAVID, V. G. REGIONAL LINGUISTIC ATLASES IN THE UNITED STATES, ORBIS, V (JUNE, 1956), 349–386.

McDAVID, R. I., JR. AND McDAVID, V. G. THE RELATIONSHIP OF THE SPEECH OF AMERICAN NEGROES TO THE SPEECH OF WHITES, AMERICAN SPEECH XXVI 1951, PP. 3–17.

McDAVID, R. I., JR. HISTORICAL, REGIONAL, AND SOCIAL VARIATION, JOURNAL OF ENGLISH LINGUISTICS, 1967, P. 39.

McDAVID, V. G. VERB FORMS IN THE NORTH-CENTRAL STATES AND THE UPPER MIDWEST, DOCTORAL DISSERTATION, UNIVERSITY OF MINNESOTA, 1956 MICROFILM.

MEADER, C. L. AND MUYSKENS, J. H. HANDBOOK OF BIOLINGUISTICS, 2ND ED., NEW YORK, HOLT, RINEHART AND WINSTON, INC., 1962, PART 1.

MECHAM, M. J., JEX, J. L., AND JONES, J. D. UTAH TEST OF LANGUAGE DEVELOPMENT, SALT LAKE CITY, COMMUNICATION RESEARCH ASSOCIATES, 1967.

MENCKEN, H. L. THE AMERICAN LANGUAGE, ABRIDGED AND EDITED BY R. I. MCDAVID, JR., NEW YORK, A. A. KNOPF, 1963.

MENYUK, P. SYNTACTIC STRUCTURES IN THE LANGUAGE OF CHILDREN, CHILD DEVELOPMENT, 1963, 34, 407–422.

MENYUK, P. SYNTACTIC RULES USED BY CHILDREN FROM PRESCHOOL THROUGH FIRST GRADE, CHILD DEVELOPMENT, 1964, 35, 533–546.

MENYUK, P. COMPARISON OF GRAMMAR OF CHILDREN WITH FUNCTIONALLY DEVIANT AND NORMAL SPEECH, JOURNAL OF SPEECH AND HEARING RESEARCH, 1964, 7, 109–121.

MENYUK, P. CUES USED IN SPEECH PERCEPTION AND PRODUCTION BY CHILDREN, QUARTERLY PROGRESS REPORT, NO. 77, RESEARCH LABORATORY OF ELECTRONICS, M. I. T., CAMBRIDGE, MASS., 1965.

MICKLESON, L. R. FORM CLASSES STRUCTURAL LINGUISTICS AND MECHANICAL TRANSLATION FOR ROMAN JAKOBSON, THE HAGUE, MOUTON AND COMPANY, 1956.

MILISEN, R. A RATIONAL FOR ARTICULATION DISORDERS, JOURNAL OF SPEECH AND HEARING DISORDERS, MONOGRAPH SUPPLEMENT, NO. 4, DECEMBER, 1954.

MILISEN, R. ET. AL., THE DISORDERS OF ARTICULATION A SYSTEMATIC

CLINICAL AND EXPERIMENTAL APPROACH, JOURNAL OF SPEECH AND HEARING DISORDERS, MONOGRAPH SUPPLEMENT, NO. 4, DECEMBER, 1954.

MILLER, D. AND SWANSON, G. EXPRESSIVE STYLES III, TWO STYLES OF EXPRESSION MOTORIC AND CONCEPTUAL, CHAPTER 15 IN MILLER AND SWANSON, INNER CONFLICT AND DEFENSE, NEW YORK, HOLT, RINEHART AND WINSTON, 1959, 337–352.

MILLER, G. A. AND NICELY, P. E. AN ANALYSIS OF PERCEPTUAL CONFUSIONS AMONG SOME ENGLISH CONSONANTS, JOURNAL OF THE ACOUSTICAL SOCIETY OF AMERICA, 27, 338–352 (1955).

MILLER, G. A. LANGUAGE AND COMMUNICATION, NEW YORK, MCGRAW-HILL BOOK COMPANY, 1951.

MILLER, G. THE PERCEPTION OF SPEECH FOR ROMAN JAKOBSON, MORRIS HALLE, ET AL., EDS., THE HAGUE, MOUTON AND COMPANY, 1956.

MILLER, G. AND NICELY, P. E. AN ANALYSIS OF PERCEPTIONAL CONFUSIONS AMONG SOME ENGLISH CONSONANTS, PSYCHOLINGUISTICS, SOL SAPORTA, ED., NEW YORK, HOLT, RINEHART AND WINSTON, INC., 1961.

MILLER, W. AND ERWIN, S. THE DEVELOPMENT OF GRAMMAR IN CHILD LANGUAGE, CHILD DEVELOPMENT MONOGRAMS, 29, 9–34, 1964.

MILLS, R. V. OREGON SPEECHWAYS, AMERICAN SPEECH, XXV (MAY, 1950), 81–90.

MILNER, E. A STUDY OF THE RELATIONSHIP BETWEEN READING READINESS IN GRADE ONE SCHOOL CHILDREN AND PATTERNS OF PARENT-CHILD INTERACTION, CHILD DEVELOPMENT, 1951, 22, 95–112.

MINIFIE, F. DARLEY, F., AND SHERMAN, D. TEMPORAL RELIABILITY OF SEVEN LANGUAGE MEASURES, JOURNAL OF SPEECH AND HEARING RESEARCH, 1963, 6, 139–148.

MITFORD, N. ED. NOBLESSE OBLIGE AN ENQUIRY INTO THE IDENTIFIABLE CHARACTERISTICS OF THE ENGLISH ARISTOCRACY, LONDON, 1956.

MOHRMANN, C., SOMMERFELT, A. AND WHATMOUGH, J. TRENDS IN EUROPEAN AND AMERICAN LINGUSTICS, UTRECHT, 1961.

MOULTON, W. G. A LINGUISTIC GUIDE TO LANGUAGE LEARNING, NEW YORK, MODERN LANGUAGE ASSOCIATION, 1966.

MOULTON, W. G. A LINGUISTIC GUIDE TO LANGUAGE LEARNING, NEW YORK, MODERN LANGUAGE ASSOCIATION, 1966.

MOULTON, W. G. THE SOUNDS OF ENGLISH AND GERMAN, CHICAGO, THE UNIVERSITY OF CHICAGO PRESS, 1962.

MOWRER, O. H. HEARING AND SPEAKING, AN ANALYSIS OF LANGUAGE LEARNING, JOURNAL OF SPEECH AND HEARING DISORDERS, XXIII, MAY, 1958, 143–52.

MOWRER, O. H. SPEECH DEVELOPMENT IN THE YOUNG CHILD, JOURNAL OF SPEECH AND HEARING DISORDERS, XVII, SEPTEMBER, 1952, 263–68.

MOWRER, O. H. THE PSYCHOLOGIST LOOKS AT LANGUAGE, AMERICAN PSYCHOLOGIST, IX, 1954, 660–92.

MOWRER, O. H. LEARNING THEORY AND THE SYMBOLIC PROCESSES, NEW YORK, JOHN WILEY, 1960.

MUKERJI, R. AND ROBISON, H.

A HEAD START IN LANGUAGE, ELEMENTARY ENGLISH, 1966, 43, 460–463.

MUNN, R. F. THE SOUTHERN APPALACHIANS, A BIBLIOGRAPHY AND GUIDE TO STUDIES, MORGANTOWN, WEST VIRGINIA UNIVERSITY LIBRARY, 1961.

MYKLEBUST, H. THE DIFFERENTIAL DIAGNOSIS OF DEAFNESS IN YOUNG CHILDREN, JOURNAL OF EXCEPTIONAL CHILDREN, XVII, 1951.

MYSAK, E. D. ORGANISMIC DEVELOPMENT OF ORAL LANGUAGE, JOURNAL OF SPEECH AND HEARING DISORDERS, XXVI, 1961, NO. 4, 377–84.

NANCE, L. S. DIFFERENTIAL DIAGNOSIS OF APHASIA, JOURNAL OF SPEECH AND HEARING DISORDERS, XI, SEPTEMBER, 1946.

NEWMAN, J. B. THE CATEGORIZATION OF DISORDERS OF SPEECH, LANGUAGE AND COMMUNICATION, JOURNAL OF SPEECH AND HEARING DISORDERS, XXVII, 1962, NO. 3, 287–89.

NEWMAN, S. S. ON THE STRESS SYSTEM OF ENGLISH, WORD, II, DECEMBER, 1946.

NEWTON, E. SECTION B, VERBAL DESTITUTION, THE PIVOTAL BARRIER TO LEARNING, JOURNAL OF NEGRO EDUCATION, 1960, 29, 497–499.

NEWTON, E. SECTION D, THE CULTURALLY DEPRIVED CHILD IN OUR VERBAL SCHOOLS, JOURNAL OF NEGRO EDUCATION, 1962, 31, 184–187.

NEWTON, E. PLANNING FOR THE LANGUAGE DEVELOPMENT OF DISADVANTAGED CHILDREN AND YOUTH, JOURNAL OF NEGRO EDUCATION, 1964, 33, 210–217.

NIDA, E. A. MORPHOLOGY, THE DESCRIPTIVE ANALYSIS OF WORDS, 2ND ED., ANN ARBOR, MICH., UNIVERSITY OF MICH. PRESS, 1962.

NISBET, J. FAMILY ENVIRONMENT AND INTELLIGENCE, HALSEY, A. H., FLOUD, J., AND ANDERSON, G. A., EDS., EDUCATION, ECONOMY AND SOCIETY, GLENCOE, ILL., FREE PRESS, 1961, 273–287.

NOEL, D. A COMPARATIVE STUDY OF THE RELATIONSHIP BETWEEN THE QUALITY OF THE CHILD'S LANGUAGE USAGE AND THE QUALITY AND TYPES OF LANGUAGE USED IN THE HOME, JOURNAL OF EDUCATIONAL RESEARCH, 1953, 47, 161–167.

O'HARE, T. J. THE LINGUISTIC GEOGRAPHY OF EASTERN MONTANA, DOCTORAL DISSERTATION, UNIVERSITY OF TEXAS, 1964, MICROFILM.

ORTON, H. AND DIETH, E. SURVEY OF ENGLISH DIALECTS, LEEDS, E. J. ARNOLD AND SON, LTD., 1962.

OSBORN, S. S. CONCEPTS OF SPEECH DEVELOPMENT, JOURNAL OF SPEECH AND HEARING DISORDERS, XXVI, 1961, NO. 4, 390–92.

OWENS, B. A. FOLK SPEECH OF THE CUMBERLANDS, AMERICAN SPEECH VII, 1931, PP. 89–95.

PALMER, H. E. ENGLISH INTONATION, W. HEFFER AND SONS, CAMBRIDGE, ENGLAND, 1922.

PALMER, H. E. AND BLANDFORD, W. G. A GRAMMAR OF SPOKEN ENGLISH, REVISED ED., W. HEFFER AND SONS, CAMBRIDGE, ENGLAND, 1939.

PARATORE, A. ENGLISH DIALOGUES FOR FOREIGN STUDENTS, NEW YORK, HOLT, RINEHART AND WINSTON, INC., 1957.

PEARCE, T. M. THREE ROCKY MOUNTAIN TERMS PARK, SUGAN AND PLAZA,

AMERICAN SPEECH, XXXIII (MAY, 1958), 99–107.

PEDERSON, L. SOCIAL DIALECTS AND THE DISADVANTAGED, IN R. CORBIN AND M. CROSBY (EDS.), LANGUAGE PROGRAMS FOR THE DISADVANTAGED CHAMPAIGN, ILL., 1965, NATIONAL COUNCIL OF TEACHERS OF ENGLISH.

PEISACH, E. CHILDREN'S COMPREHENSION OF TEACHER AND PEER SPEECH, CHILD DEVELOPMENT, 1965, 36, 467–480.

PEI, M. ONE LANGUAGE FOR THE WORLD, NEW YORK, THE DEVIN-ADAIR COMPANY, 1958.

PERRY, L. S. A STUDY OF THE PRONOUN HIT IN GRASSY BRANCH, NORTH CAROLINA.

PETERS, R. W. DIMENSION OF QUALITY FOR THE VOWEL AE, JOURNAL OF SPEECH AND HEARING RESEARCH, VI, SEPTEMBER, 1963.

PETTIGREW, T. F. A PROFILE OF THE NEGRO AMERICAN, PRINCETON, D. VAN NOSTRAND, 1964.

PFAFF, P. L. THE MOTO-KINESTHETIC METHOD APPLIED TO APHASICS, JOURNAL OF SPEECH AND HEARING DISORDERS, V, SEPTEMBER, 1940.

PIAGET, J. THE LANGUAGE AND THOUGHT OF THE CHILD, NEW YORK, MERIDIAN BOOKS, INC., 1959.

PIERIS, R. SPEECH AND SOCIETY, A SOCIOLOGICAL APPROACH TO LANGUAGE, AMERICAN SOCIOLOGICAL REVIEW, 1951, 16, 499–505.

PIKE, K. L. THE INTONATION OF AMERICAN ENGLISH, UNIVERSITY OF MICHIGAN, ANN ARBOR, MICH., 1945.

PRATOR, C. MANUAL OF AMERICAN ENGLISH PRONUNCIATION, REV. ED., NEW YORK, HOLT, RINEHART AND WINSTON, INC., 1957.

PREHM, H. CONCEPT LEARNING IN CULTURALLY DISADVANTAGED CHILDREN AS A FUNCTION OF VERBAL PRE-TRAINING, EXCEPTIONAL CHILDREN, 1966, 32, 599–604.

PUTNAM, G. N. AND O'HERN, E. THE STATUS SIGNIFICANCE OF AN ISOLATED URBAN DIALECT, LANGUAGE DISSERTATION NO. 53, LANGUAGE, 1955, 31, NO. 4, WHOLE PART 2.

PYLES, T. WORDS AND WAYS OF AMERICAN ENGLISH, NEW YORK, RANDOM HOUSE, INC., 1952.

QUIRK, R. R. THE USE OF ENGLISH, NEW YORK, 1962.

RACKSTRAW, S. J. AND ROBINSON, W. P. SOCIAL AND PSYCHOLOGICAL FACTORS RELATED TO VARIABILITY OF ANSWERING BEHAVIOR IN FIVE-YEAR-OLD CHILDREN, LANGUAGE AND SPEECH, 1967, 10, 88–106.

RADIN, N. AND KAMII, C. THE CHILD-REARING ATTITUDES OF DISADVANTAGED NEGRO MOTHERS AND SOME EDUCATIONAL IMPLICATIONS, JOURNAL OF NEGRO EDUCATION, 1965, 34, 138–146.

RANDOLPH, V. THE GRAMMAR OF THE OZARK DIALECT, AMERICAN SPEECH II, 1927, PP. 1–11.

RANDOLPH, V. AND INGLEMANN, A. A. PRONUNCIATION IN THE OZARK DIALECT, AMERICAN SPEECH III, 1928, PP. 401–407.

RANDOLPH, V. AND SANKEE, P. DIALECTAL SURVIVALS IN THE OZARKS I. ARCHAIC PRONUNCIATION, AMERICAN SPEECH V, 1930, PP. 198–208.

RANDOLPH, V. AND SANKEE, P. DIALECTAL SURVIVALS IN THE OZARKS

II, GRAMMATICAL PARTICULARITIES, AMERICAN SPEECH V, 1930, PP. 264–269.

RANDOLPH, V. AND SANKEE, P. DIALECTAL SURVIVALS IN THE OZARKS III, ARCHAIC VOCABULARY, AMERICAN SPEECH V, 1930, PP. 424–430.

RAO, G. S. INDIAN WORDS IN ENGLISH, OXFORD, 1954.

RAPH, J. LANGUAGE DEVELOPMENT IN SOCIALLY DISADVANTAGED CHILDREN, REVIEW OF EDUCATION RESEARCH, 1965, 35, 389–400.

REED, C. E. THE PRONUNCIATION OF ENGLISH IN THE STATE OF WASHINGTON, AMERICAN SPEECH, XXVII (OCT., 1952), 186–189.

REED, C. E. WASHINGTON WORDS, PUBLICATION OF THE AMERICAN DIALECT SOCIETY, NO. 25 (APRIL, 1956), 3–11.

REED, C. E. WORD GEOGRAPHY OF THE PACIFIC NORTHWEST, ORBIS, VI (JAN.–JUNE, 1957), 82–89.

REED, C. E. FRONTIERS OF ENGLISH IN THE PACIFIC NORTHWEST, PROCEEDINGS OF THE 9TH PACIFIC NORTHWEST CONFERENCE OF FOREIGN LANGUAGE TEACHERS (APRIL, 1958), PP. 33–35.

REED, C. E. THE PRONUNCIATION OF ENGLISH IN THE PACIFIC NORTHWEST, LANGUAGE, XXVII (OCT.–DEC., 1961), 559–564.

REED, D. W. EASTERN DIALECT WORDS IN CALIFORNIA, PUBLICATION OF THE AMERICAN DIALECT SOCIETY, NO. 21 (1954), PP. 3–15.

REINECKE, J. E. PIDGIN ENGLISH IN HAWAII, A LOCAL STUDY IN THE SOCIOLOGY OF LANGUAGE, AMERICAN JOURNAL OF SOCIOLOGY, 1938, 43, 778–789.

REVTOVA, L. D. THE INTONATION OF DECLARATIVE SENTENCES IN CURRENT ENGLISH AND RUSSIAN, PRESENTED AT THE 5TH INTERNATIONAL CONGRESS OF PHONETIC SCIENCE, MUNSTER, GERMANY, AUGUST, 16–22, 1964.

RICE, D. B. AND MILISEN, R. THE INFLUENCE OF INCREASED STIMULATION UPON THE PRODUCTION OF UNFAMILIAR SOUNDS AS A FUNCTION OF TIME, JOURNAL OF SPEECH AND HEARING DISORDERS, MONOGRAPH SUPPLEMENT, NO. 4, DECEMBER, 1959.

RIESSMAN, F. AND ALBERTS, F. DIGGING 'THE MAN'S' LANGUAGE, SATURDAY REVIEW OF LITERATURE, SEPT. 17, 1966, 80–81, 98.

ROBERTS, P. UNDERSTANDING ENGLISH, NEW YORK, 1958.

ROBINSON, W. P. CLOZE PROCEDURE AS A TECHNIQUE FOR THE INVESTIGATION OF SOCIAL CLASS DIFFERENCES IN LANGUAGE USAGE, LANGUAGE AND SPEECH, 1965, 8, 42–55.

ROBINSON, W. P. THE ELABORATED CODE IN WORKING CLASS LANGUAGE, LANGUAGE AND SPEECH, 1965, 8, 243–252.

ROJAS, P. AMERICAN ENGLISH SERIES, TEACHERS GUIDE BOOKS 1 AND 2, NEW YORK, D. C. HEATH AND CO., 1952.

ROMEO, A. THE LANGUAGE OF GANGS, UNPUBLISHED MANUSCRIPT, MOBILIZATION FOR YOUTH, (214 E. SECOND ST.), N. Y.

ROSTEN, L. THE EDUCATION OF HYMAN KAPLAN, NEW YORK, HARCOURT, BRACE AND WORLD, INC., 1937.

ROSTEN, L. THE RETURN OF HYMAN KAPLAN, NEW YORK, HARPER AND ROW, PUBLISHERS, INC., 1959.

RUESCH, J. AND KEES, W. NONVER-
BAL COMMUNICATION, BERKELEY,
UNIVERSITY OF CALIFORNIA PRESS,
1956.

RUESCH, J. DISTURBED COMMUNICA-
TION, NEW YORK, W. W. NORTON AND
COMPANY, INC., 1957.

SARETT, L., FOSTER, W. T., AND
SARETT, A. J. BASIC PRINCIPLES OF
SPEECH, 3RD ED., BOSTON, HOUGHTON
MIFFLIN COMPANY, 1958.

SCARGILL, M. H. SOURCES OF CANA-
DIAN ENGLISH, JOURNAL OF ENGLISH
AND GERMANIC PHILOLOGY, LVI
(OCT., 1957), 610–614.

SCHATZMAN, L. AND STRAUSS, A.
SOCIAL CLASS AND MODES OF COM-
MUNICATION, AMERICAN JOURNAL OF
SOCIOLOGY, 1955, 69, 329–338.

SCHUBIGER, M. THE ROLE OF INTO-
NATION IN SPOKEN ENGLISH, W. HEF-
FER AND SONS, CAMBRIDGE, ENGLAND,
1935.

SCHUBIGER, M. ENGLISH INTONA-
TION, ITS FORM AND FUNCTION, MAX
NIEMEYER, TUBINGEN, 1958.

SEQUENTIAL TESTS OF EDUCATIONAL
PROGRESS-LISTENING, LOS ANGELES,
COOPERATIVE TESTING SERVICE, 1957.

SERJEANTSON, M. S. A HISTORY OF
FOREIGN WORDS IN ENGLISH, LONDON,
1935.

SHANNON, C. AND WEAVER, W.
THE MATHEMATICAL THEORY OF
COMMUNICATION, URBANA, UNIVER-
SITY OF ILLINOIS PRESS, 1949.

SHEARER, L. AMERICANS WHO CAN'T
SPEAK THEIR OWN LANGUAGE, PA-
RADE, JUNE 11, 1967, 6–7.

SHEEHAN, J. G. AN INTEGRATION OF
PSYCHOTHERAPY AND SPEECH THER-
APY THROUGH A CONFLICT THEORY

OF STUTTERING, JOURNAL OF SPEECH
AND HEARING DISORDERS, XIX, DECEM-
BER, 1954, 474–82.

SHEN, Y. INITIAL R IN AMERICAN
ENGLISH AND MANDARIN CHINESE AND
HOW TO TEACH IT, LANGUAGE LEARN-
ING, II, NO. 2, APRIL–JUNE, 1949.

SIGEL, I., ANDERSON, L., AND
SHAPIRO, H. CATEGORIZATION BE-
HAVIOR OF LOWER- AND MIDDLE-
CLASS NEGRO PRESCHOOL CHILDREN,
DIFFERENCES IN DEALING WITH REP-
RESENTATION OF FAMILIAR OBJECTS,
JOURNAL OF NEGRO EDUCATION,
1966, 35, 218–229.

SILLER, J. SOCIOECONOMIC STATUS
AND CONCEPTUAL THINKING, THE
JOURNAL OF ARNORMAL AND SOCIAL
PSYCHOLOGY, 1957, 55, 365–371.

SIMON, C. T. COMPLEXITY AND
BREAKDOWN IN SPEECH SITUATION,
JOURNAL OF SPEECH DISORDERS, X,
SEPTEMBER, 1945, 199–203.

SINNOTT, E. W. MATTER, MIND AND
MAN, LONDON, G. ALLEN AND UNWIN,
1958.

SINNOTT, E. W. PLANT MORPHO-
GENESIS, NEW YORK, MCGRAW-HILL
BOOK COMPANY, 1960.

SKEAT, W. W. (ED.), AN ETYMOLO-
GICAL DICTIONARY OF THE ENGLISH
LANGUAGE, OXFORD, 1882.

SKEAT, W. W. ENGLISH DIALECTS
FROM THE EIGHTH CENTURY TO THE
PRESENT DAY, CAMBRIDGE, ENGLAND,
1911.

SLAGER, W., ED., ENGLISH FOR TO-
DAY, THE NATIONAL COUNCIL OF
TEACHERS OF ENGLISH, NEW YORK,
THE MCGRAW-HILL BOOK CO., 1962.

SMILEY, M. RESEARCH AND ITS IM-
PLICATIONS, IN A. JEWETT, J. MER-

SAND AND D. GUNDERSON, IMPROVING ENGLISH SKILLS OF CULTURALLY DIFFERENT YOUTH, WASHINGTON, D. C., U. S. GOVERNMENT PRINTING OFFICE.

SMITH, J. AND LINN, J. R. SKILL IN ORAL READING, NEW YORK, HARPER AND ROW, PUBLISHERS, INC., 1960.

SPEECH COMMITTEE OF THE DEPARTMENT OF ENGLISH, MANUAL OF ORAL ENGLISH EXERCISES, ENGLISH 105, RIO RIEDRAS, P. R., PUERTO RICO UNIVERSITY, 1959–1960.

STETSON, R. H. MOTOR PHONETICS, A STUDY OF SPEECH MOVEMENTS IN ACTION, 2ND ED., AMSTERDAM, NORTH-HOLLAND PUBLISHING CO., FOR OBERLIN COLLEGE, 1951.

STEVENS, C., BRONSTEIN, A. J., AND WONG, H. H. ENGLISH AS A SECOND LANGUAGE—PRACTICES OF SPEECH DEPARTMENTS, QUARTERLY JOURNAL OF SPEECH, XLVIII, OCTOBER, 1962, NO. 3, 285–96.

STEVENS, K. N. AND HALLE, M. REMARKS ON ANALYSIS-BY-SYNTHESIS AND DISTINCTIVE FEATURES, PROCEEDINGS OF SYMPOSIUM ON MODELS FOR THE PERCEPTION OF SPEECH AND VISUAL FORM, BOSTON, MASS., 1964.

STEVENS, K. N. AND HOUSE, A. S. PERTURBATION OF VOWEL ARTICULATIONS BY CONSONANTAL CONTEXT, AN ACOUSTICAL STUDY, JOURNAL OF SPEECH AND HEARING RESEARCH, VI, JUNE, 1963.

STEWART, J. THE PROBLEM OF STUTTERING IN CERTAIN NORTH AMERICAN INDIAN SOCIETIES, MONOGRAPH SUPPLEMENT NO. 6, JOURNAL OF SPEECH AND HEARING DISORDERS, 1960.

STEWART, W. A. URBAN NEGRO SPEECH, SOCIOLINGUISTIC FACTORS AFFECTING ENGLISH TEACHING, SHUY, R., ED., SOCIAL DIALECTS AND LANGUAGE LEARNING, CHAMPAIGN, ILLINOIS, NATIONAL COUNCIL OF TEACHERS OF ENGLISH, 1965.

STEWART, W. A. FOREIGN LANGUAGE TEACHING METHODS IN QUASI-FOREIGN LANGUAGE SITUATIONS, STEWART, W. A., ED., NON-STANDARD SPEECH AND THE TEACHING OF ENGLISH, WASHINGTON, D. C., THE CENTER FOR APPLIED LINGUISTICS, 1964.

STEWART, W. A. URBAN NEGRO SPEECH, SOCIOLINGUISTIC FACTORS AFFECTING ENGLISH TEACHING, SHUY, R. W., ED., SOCIAL DIALECTS AND LANGUAGE LEARNING, CHAMPAIGN, ILL., NATIONAL COUNCIL OF TEACHERS OF ENGLISH, 1965.

STEWART, W. A. SOCIOLINGUISTIC FACTORS IN THE HISTORY OF AMERICAN NEGRO DIALECTS, THE FLORIDA FL REPORTER, VOL. 5, NO. 2, 1967.

STEWART, W. A. CREOLE LANGUAGES IN THE CARIBBEAN, RICE, F. A., ED., STUDY OF THE ROLE OF SECOND LANGUAGES IN ASIA, AFRICA, AND LATIN AMERICA, WASHINGTON, D. C., CENTER FOR APPLIED LINGUISTICS, 1962.

ST. ONGE, K. ARTICOLOGY, ASHA, V., JANUARY, 1963, 499.

STODOLSKY, S. MATERIAL BEHAVIOR AND LANGUAGE AND CONCEPT FORMATION IN NEGRO PRE-SCHOOL CHILDREN, AN INQUIRY INTO PROCESS, UNPUBLISHED DOCTORAL DISSERTATION, UNIVERSITY OF CHICAGO, 1965.

STRAUSS, A. AND SCHATZMAN, L. CROSS-CLASS INTERVIEWING, AN ANALYSIS OF INTERACTION AND COMMUNI-

CATIVE STYLES, HUMAN ORGANIZA-TION, 1955, 14, 28–31.

STODTBECK, F. L. THE HIDDEN CURRICULUM IN THE MIDDLE-CLASS HOME, IN J. D. KRUMBOLTZ (ED.), LEARNING AND THE EDUCATIONAL PROCESS, CHICAGO, RAND MCNALLY, 1965, 91–112.

STROUD, R. A STUDY OF THE RELA-TIONS BETWEEN SOCIAL DISTANCE AND SPEECH DIFFERENCES OF WHITE AND NEGRO HIGH SCHOOL STUDENTS OF DAYTON, OHIO, MASTER'S THESIS, BOWLING GREEN STATE UNIVERSITY (1961).

TABA, H. CULTURAL DEPRIVATION AS A FACTOR IN SCHOOL LEARNING, MER-RILL-PALMER QUARTERLY, 1964, 10, 147–159.

TAYLOR, D. LANGUAGE SHIFT OR CHANGING RELATIONSHIPS, INTERNA-TIONAL JOURNAL OF AMERICAN LIN-GUISTICS, 26 2 1950.

TEMPLIN, M. RELATION OF SPEECH AND LANGUAGE DEVELOPMENT TO IN-TELLIGENCE AND SOCIO-ECONOMIC STATUS, VOLTA REVIEW, 1958, 60, 331–334.

TEMPLIN, M. CERTAIN LANGUAGE SKILLS IN CHILDREN, INSTITUTE OF CHILD WELFARE MONOGRAPH SERIES NO. 26, MINNEAPOLIS, MINN., 1957, UNIVERSITY OF MINNESOTA PRESS.

TEMPLIN, M. A STUDY OF SOUND DIS-CRIMINATION ABILITY OF ELEMEN-TARY SCHOOL PUPILS, JOURNAL OF SPEECH DISORDERS, VIII, 1943.

TEMPLIN, M. AND DARLEY, F. L. THE TEMPLIN-DARLEY TEST OF ARTIC-ULATION, IOWA CITY, IOWA, BUREAU OF EDUCATIONAL RESEARCH AND SER-VICE EXTENSION DIVISION, STATE UNI-VERSITY OF IOWA, 1960.

TENG, SSU-YU CONVERSATIONAL CHINESE, CHICAGO, UNIVERSITY OF CHICAGO PRESS, 1952.

TERREL, G., JR., DURKIN, K., AND WIESLEY, M. SOCIAL CLASS AND THE NATURE OF THE INCENTIVE IN DISCRIMINATION LEARNING, JOUR-NAL OF ABNORMAL AND SOCIAL PSY-CHOLOGY, 59, 270–272, (1959).

THE MARCH OF CIVILIZATION IN MAPS AND PICTURES, NEW YORK, C. S. HAM-MOND AND CO., INC., 1957.

THOMAS, C. K. THE DIALECTAL SIG-NIFICANCE OF THE NON-PHONEMIC LOW-BACK VOWEL VARIANTS BEFORE R, STUDIES IN SPEECH AND DRAMA IN HONOR OF ALEXANDER M. DRUM-MOND, ITHACA, NEW YORK, 1944.

THOMAS, C. K. AN INTRODUCTION TO THE PHONETICS OF AMERICAN ENG-LISH, REV. ED., NEW YORK, THE RONALD PRESS, 1958.

THOMAS, C. K. CHINESE DIFFICUL-TIES WITH ENGLISH PRONUNCIATIONS, JOURNAL OF SPEECH AND HEARING DISORDERS, IV, SEPTEMBER, 1939.

THOMAS, D. R. ORAL LANGUAGE, SENTENCE STRUCGURE, AND VOCABU-LARY OF KINDERGARTEN CHILDREN LIVING IN LOW SOCIO-ECONOMIC UR-BAN AREAS, UNPUBLISHED DOCTORAL DISSERTATION, WAYNE STATE UNIVER-SITY, 1962.

TRAGER, G. L. AND SMITH, H. L., JR. AN OUTLINE OF ENGLISH STRUC-TURE STUDIES IN LINGUISTICS, OCCA-SIONAL PAPERS, NO. 3, NORMAN, OKLA., BATTENBURG PRESS, 1951.

TRAGER, G. L. LINGUISTICS, ENCY-

CLOPEDIA BRITANNICA, 1961, VOL. 14, 163–171.

TRAVIS, L. E., JOHNSON, W. AND SHOVER, J. THE RELATION OF BILINGUALISM TO STUTTERING, JOURNAL OF SPEECH DISORDERS, II, 1937, 185.

TRAVIS, L. E. HANDBOOK OF SPEECH PATHOLOGY, NEW YORK, APPLETON-CENTURY-CROFTS, 1957.

TRAVIS, L. E. AND RASMUS, B. THE SPEECH SOUND DISCRIMINATION ABILITY OF CASES WITH FUNCTIONAL DISORDERS OF ARTICULATION, QUARTERLY JOURNAL OF SPEECH, XVII, 1931.

TUCKER, M. F. LISTENING LESSONS IN CONNECTED SPEECH FOR PUERTO RICAN COLLEGE STUDENTS FOR THE PURPOSE OF IMPROVING AURAL COMPREHENSION IN ENGLISH, UNPUBLISHED MASTER'S THESIS, UNIVERSITY OF NEW MEXICO, 1963.

TURNER, L. D. NOTES ON THE SOUNDS AND VOCABULARY OF GULLAH, PUBLICATION OF THE AMERICAN DIALECT SOCIETY, NO. 3 (1945), PP. 13–28.

TURNER, L. D. AFRICANISMS IN THE GULLAH DIALECT, CHICAGO, 1949.

UPTON, A. DESIGN FOR THINKING, STANFORD, CALIF., STANFORD UNIVERSITY PRESS, 1961.

VAN RIPER, C. SPEECH CORRECTION, PRINCIPLES AND METHODS, 4TH ED., ENGLEWOOD CLIFFS, N. J., PRENTICE-HALL, INC., 1963.

VAN RIPER, C. TEACHING YOUR CHILD TO TALK, NEW YORK, HARPER AND ROW, PUBLISHERS, 1950.

VAN RIPER, C. AND SMITH, D. E. AN INTRODUCTION TO GENERAL AMERICAN PHONETICS, 2ND ED., NEW YORK, HARPER AND ROW, PUBLISHERS, 1962.

VAN RIPER, C. AND IRWIN, J. V. VOICE AND ARTICULATION, ENGLEWOOD CLIFFS, N. J., PRENTICE-HALL, INC., 1958.

VERNON, P. E. ABILITY FACTORS AND ENVIRONMENTAL INFLUENCES, THE AMERICAN PSYCHOLOGIST, 1965, 20, 723–733.

VIGOTSKY, L. S. THOUGHT AND SPEECH, PSYCHIATRY, II, 1939.

WEBSTER'S NEW COLLEGIATE DICTIONARY, SPRINGFIELD, MASS., G. AND C. MERRIAM COMPANY.

WEINREICH, U. LANGUAGES IN CONTACT FINDINGS AND PROBLEMS, NEW YORK, THE LINGUISTIC CIRCLE OF NEW YORK, 1953.

WELLER, J. E. YESTERDAY'S PEOPLE, LIFE IN CONTEMPORARY APPALACHIA, LEXINGTON, UNIVERSITY OF KENTUCKY PRESS, 1966.

WELLS, R. S. THE PITCH PHONEMES OF ENGLISH, LANGUAGE, 21, 27–40, 1945.

WELTY, J. C. THE LIFE OF BIRDS, PHILADELPHIA, W. B. SAUNDERS CO., 1962, PP. 204–8.

WENDAHL, R. W. AND COLE, J. IDENTIFICATION OF STUTTERING DURING RELATIVELY FLUENT SPEECH, JOURNAL OF SPEECH AND HEARING RESEARCH, IV, SEPTEMBER, 1961.

WENTWORTH, H. (ED.), AMERICAN DIALECT DICTIONARY, NEW YORK, 1944.

WESTOVER, J. H. HIGHLAND LANGUAGE OF THE CUMBERLAND COAL COUNTRY, MOUNTAIN LIFE AND WORK XXXVI, NO. 3, 1960, PP. 18–21.

WETMORE, T. H. THE LOW-CEN-

TRAL AND LOW-BACK VOWELS IN THE ENGLISH OF THE EASTERN UNITED STATES, PUBLICATION OF THE AMERICAN DIALECT SOCIETY, NO. 32 (1959).

WHATMOUGH, J. LANGUAGE, A MODERN SYNTHESIS, NEW YORK, THE AMERICAN BOOK LIBRARY, 1960.

WHITEHALL, H. STRUCTURAL ESSENTIALS OF ENGLISH, NEW YORK, 1956.

WHITNEY, E. ED., SYMBOLOGY, THE USE OF VISUAL SYMBOLS IN VISUAL COMMUNICATION, NEW YORK, HASTINGS HOUSE PUBLISHERS, INC., 1960.

WHORF, B. L. THE RELATION OF HABITUAL THOUGHT AND BEHAVIOR TO LANGUAGE, LANGUAGE, CULTURE AND PERSONALITY, LESLIE SPIER, ET AL., EDS., MENASHA, WIS., SAPIR MEMORIAL PUBLICATION FUND, 1941., PP. 75–93.

WHORF, B. L. LANGUAGES, THOUGHT AND REALITY, BOSTON, MASS., MASS. INSTITUTE OF TECHNOLOGY PRESS, WITH J. WILEY AND SONS, INC., 1956.

WHORF, B. L. THE RELATION OF HABITUAL THOUGHT AND BEHAVIOR TO LANGUAGE, LANGUAGE, CULTURE AND PERSONALITY, L. SPIER, ET AL., EDS., KENOSHA, WIS., SAPIR MEMORIAL PUBLICATION FUND, 1941.

WHORF, B. L. SCIENCE AND LINGUISTICS, READINGS IN APPLIED LINGUISTICS, NEW YORK, APPLETON-CENTURY-CROFTS, 1958.

WILLIAMS, E. R. CONTACTS OF NEGROES AND WHITE IN MORGANTOWN, THESIS, WEST VIRGINIA UNIVERSITY, 1952.

WILLIAMS, C. D. THE R IN MOUNTAIN SPEECH, MOUNTAIN LIFE AND WORK, XXXVII, NO. 1, 1961, PP. 5–8.

WILLIAMS, C. D. RHYTHM AND MELODY IN MOUNTAIN SPEECH, MOUNTAIN LIFE AND WORK, XXXVII, NO. 3, 1961, PP. 7–10.

WILLIAMS, C. D. THE CONTENT OF MOUNTAIN SPEECH, MOUNTAIN LIFE AND WORK, XXXVII, NO. 4, 1961, PP. 13–17.

WILLIAMS, C. D. MOUNTAINEERS MIND THEIR MANNERS, MOUNTAIN LIFE AND WORK, XXXVII, NO. 2, 1962, PP. 15–19.

WILLIAMS, C. D. METAPHOR IN MOUNTAIN SPEECH, MOUNTAIN LIFE AND WORK, XXXVII, NO. 4, 1962, PP. 9–12.

WILLIAMS, C. D. METAPHOR IN MOUNTAIN SPEECH, MOUNTAIN LIFE AND WORK, XXXIX, NO. 2, 1963, PP. 51–53.

WILLIAMS, C. D. PREPOSITIONS IN MOUNTAIN SPEECH, MOUNTAIN LIFE AND WORK, XL, NO. 1, 1964, PP. 53–55.

WILLIAMS, C. D. SUBTLETY IN MOUNTAIN SPEECH, MOUNTAIN LIFE AND WORK, XLIII, NO. 1, 1967, PP. 14–16.

WILLIAMS, J. J. AND SURLA, L. T., JR. THE INCIDENCE OF POVERTY, 2ND EDITION, NASHVILLE, TENNESSEE, STATE PLANNING COMMISSION, 1965.

WILSON, C. M. BACKWOODS AMERICA, CHAPEL HILL, THE UNIVERSITY OF NORTH CAROLINA PRESS, 1934.

WILSON, H. R. THE DIALECT OF LUNENBURG COUNTY, NOVA SCOTIA, DOCTORAL DISSERTATION, UNIVERSITY OF MICHIGAN, 1958, MICROFILM.

WINITZ, H. LANGUAGE SKILLS OF MALE AND FEMALE KINDERGARTEN CHILDREN, JOURNAL OF SPEECH AND

HEARING RESEARCH, 1959, 2, 377–386.

WINITZ, H. AND BELLROSE, B. EFFECTS OF PRETRAINING ON SOUND DISCRIMINATION LEARNING, JOURNAL OF SPEECH AND HEARING RESEARCH, VI, JUNE, 1963.

WISE, C. M. APPLIED PHONETICS, ENGLEWOOD CLIFFS, N. J., PRENTICE-HALL, INC., 1957.

WISE, C. M. INTRODUCTION TO PHONETICS, ENGLEWOOD CLIFFS, N. J., PRENTICE-HALL, INC., 1958.

WOODSON, C. G. THE RURAL NEGRO, WASHINGTON, D. C., THE ASSOCIATION FOR THE STUDY OF NEGRO LIFE AND HISTORY, 1930.

WOOD, G. R. AN ATLAS SURVEY OF THE INTERIOR SOUTH (U.S.A.), ORBIS, IX (JAN., 1960), 7–12.

WOOD, G. R. WORD DISTRIBUTION IN THE INTERIOR SOUTH, PUBLICATION OF THE AMERICAN DIALECT SOCIETY, NO. 35 (1961), 1–16.

WORTIS, H., BARDACH, J. L., CUTLER, R., RUE, R., AND FREEDMAN, A. CHILD-REARING PRACTICES IN A LOW SOCIOECONOMIC GROUP, PEDIATRICS, 1963, 32, 298–307.

WRIGHT, J. THE ENGLISH DIALECT GRAMMAR, OXFORD, 1905.

WYLD, H. C. A HISTORY OF MODERN COLLOQUIAL ENGLISH, 3RD ED., NEW YORK, 1937.

WYLD, H. C. PRONUNCIATION OF ENGLISH VOWELS, 1400–1700, GOTEBORG, SWEDEN, 1913.

YANDELL, M. D. SOME DIFFICULTIES WHICH INDIAN CHILDREN ENCOUNTER WITH IDIOMS IN READING, UNPUBLISHED MASTER'S THESIS, UNIVERSITY OF NEW MEXICO, 1959.

YERKES, R. M. CHIMPANZEE, A LABORATORY COLONY, NEW HAVEN, CONN., YALE UNIVERSITY PRESS, 1943.

YOUNG, E. H. AND HAWK, S. S. MOTO-KINESTHETIC SPEECH TRAINING, STANFORD, CALIF., STANFORD UNIVERSITY PRESS, 1955.

YOUNG, R. W. THE NAVAJO LANGUAGES, MIMEOGRAPHED EDITION PREPARED FOR THE APPENDIX OF THE 1960–61 NAVAJO YEARBOOK.

ZINTZ, M. V. EDUCATION ACROSS CULTURES, DUBUQUE, IOWA, WILLIAM C. BROWN BOOK CO., 1963.